COMPLETING GRADUATE SCHOOL LONG DISTANCE

Graduate Survival Skills

Series Editor

Bruce A. Thyer, Ph.D.
Research Professor of Social Work
University of Georgia

The volumes in this series attempt to demystify the process of earning a graduate degree. They seek to meet the need among young scholars for insights into the workings of graduate schools, from the application and admissions process through finding an academic job.

This series is targeted at readers interested in strategies for improving their experience in and with graduate school. The authors of the books come from a variety of academic disciplines, and a variety of career stages. Volumes in the series thus far include:

Surviving Graduate School Part Time
Von Pittman

The Women's Guide to Surviving Graduate School
Barbara Rittner and *Patricia Trudeau*

Completing Graduate School Long Distance
Darrel L. Hammon and *Steven K. Albiston*

Finding an Academic Job
Karen Sowers-Hoag and *Dianne F. Harrison*

The African American Student's Guide to Graduate School
Alicia Isaac

We invite ideas for future books in this series. Possible topics include:

Getting Into Graduate School, Financing Your Graduate Education, Completing Your Dissertation or Thesis, Working With Your Major Professor or Advisory Committee, Maintaining a Rewarding Personal Life as a Graduate Student, and *Handling Difficult or Sensitive Situations While in Graduate School.*

We encourage authors from all academic disciplines, and at any career stage. Potential authors can submit formal proposals (along with a current c.v.) for individual titles to the Series Editor.

COMPLETING GRADUATE SCHOOL LONG DISTANCE

Darrel L. Hammon
Steven K. Albiston

GRADUATE SURVIVAL SKILLS

SAGE Publications
International Educational and Professional Publisher
Thousand Oaks   London   New Delhi

For information:

SAGE Publications, Inc.
2455 Teller Road
Thousand Oaks, California 91320
E-mail: order@sagepub.com

SAGE Publications Ltd.
6 Bonhill Street
London EC2A 4PU
United Kingdom

SAGE Publications India Pvt. Ltd.
M-32 Market
Greater Kailash I
New Delhi 110 048 India

Printed in the United States of America

Library of Congress Cataloging-in-Publication Data

Hammon, Darrel L.
    Completing graduate school long distance / by Darrel L. Hammon,
Steven K. Albiston.
        p. cm. — (Surviving graduate school ; vol. 3)
    Includes bibliographical references and index.
    ISBN 0-7619-0486-7 (pbk.: acid-free paper). — ISBN 0-7619-0485-9
(cloth: acid-free paper)
    1. Universities and colleges—United States—Graduate work.
2. Distance education—United States. 3. University extension—
United States. I. Albiston, Steven K. II. Title. III. Series: Surviving graduate
school ; v. 3.
LB2371.4.H356 1998
378.1'55—dc21   97-21204

This book is printed on acid-free paper.

98 99 00 01 02 03 04 7 6 5 4 3 2 1

Acquiring Editor:	Jim Nageotte
Editorial Assistant:	Kathleen Derby
Production Editor:	Astrid Virding
Production Assistant:	Karen Wiley
Typesetter:	Yang-hee Maresca
Print Buyer:	Anna Chin

CONTENTS

SERIES EDITOR'S INTRODUCTION

Completing Graduate School Long Distance is a welcome addition to the **Graduate Survival Skills** series. The present volume is written by two scholars who know of what they speak, because both finished their doctorate degrees while residing several hundred miles away from their university's main campus. Graduate education provided at satellite campuses has long been around—many major universities have offered such **external degree programs** for decades. What is changing in today's graduate school environment is the increasing availability of such master's and doctoral programs, and there is a growing awareness of the potential educational quality that such programs can provide. No longer seen as higher education's pedagogical step-children, graduate degrees earned long distance from properly accredited institutions are invaluable for talented individuals fully engaged in the dynamics of life, marriage, and career, and who cannot arrange to attend a campus-based program of study. Readers of the present volume will find it extremely useful in helping them to decide to undertake and complete a master's or doctoral program long distance.

I have some personal experience in this issue, having earned my own BSc in psychology from the University of Maryland's University College program offered to military personnel serving overseas. With a previously earned AA in hand, I finished most of my junior and senior college years attending courses at night, part-time, in Okinawa, Japan, where I was stationed. I remain immensely grateful for the opportunities this long distance college program provided, and I am pleased that similarly structured graduate programs are increasingly the norm.

One very important caveat. There presently exist about half a dozen regional accrediting bodies that legitimately accredit colleges and universities. For example, my institution, the University of Georgia, is accredited by the Commission on Colleges of the Southern Association of Colleges and Schools. It is absolutely crucial that one only enroll in a graduate degree program that is itself offered from a reputable university that is properly accredited. This will be the case for almost all state and large private universities and will likely not be the case for degree-granting institutions that are not established on a larger foundation of campus-based instruction, are overseas institutions of which no one has ever heard (see Gillotte, 1997), those that grant academic credit of "life experience," or that offer master's or doctorates for a flat-rate "tuition" fee. If in doubt about the academic reputability of a potential long distance graduate degree program, consult the excellent book *Diploma Mills: Degrees of Fraud* by Stewart and Spille (1988), contact established scholars in a given field, or inquire about accreditation. So-called state approval to grant graduate degrees means little in the absence of reputable accreditation. It would be tragic to spend time and money earning an unaccredited graduate degree that is not recognized by potential employers. The National University Continuing Education Association (NUCEA, 1996) offers a comprehensive guide to 100 colleges and universities that deliver degree programs long distance, and it is also worth consulting.

The rewards following the successful completion of a graduate degree long distance can be numerous and well worth the time and effort required. Learn from the lessons of Hammon and Albiston, and try to have some fun along the way.

BRUCE A. THYER
The University of Georgia
Athens, Georgia

REFERENCES

Gillotte, T. (1997, 25 April). Thailand cracks down on diploma mills. *Chronicle of Higher Education,* p. A46.

National University Continuing Education Association. (1996). *The electronic university: A guide to distance learning programs.* Princeton, NJ: Peterson's Guides.

Stewart, D. W., & Spille, H. A. (1988). *Diploma mills: Degrees of fraud.* New York: American Council on Education.

PREFACE

This book is for those planning, exploring, or currently completing graduate school via long distance. We chose to write about this topic, completing graduate school long distance, because we participated in a doctoral program via long distance. As we were going through our doctoral program—from Idaho Falls, Idaho, to the University of Idaho, Boise Center (278 miles), to the University of Idaho, Moscow (560 miles)—we took on a different role as "distance students,"and we had many questions about what to expect. As time went on, all the questions we had were answered, and all of our anxieties dissipated. We did not want others to enroll in a long distance program with as many unanswered questions. We surveyed other graduate students who have followed the same long distance education path to help us answer the questions and give greater insight into the notion of completing a graduate program long distance.

Other books exist that discuss graduate schools on a more theoretical base, replete with academic pontifications and summations of wonderful graduate programs. The approach we wish to take in this book is an applied, emotive approach. Our primary audience is the graduate students who are seeking graduate degrees while working full- or part-time in areas that do not have a graduate school within a reasonable distance.

Because respondents to our survey have finished or will be finishing their master's and doctoral programs via long distance, it seems natural—almost imperative—that we answer and discuss the questions as we experienced them. At the beginning of each chapter, we ask numerous questions that we believe you should reflect on before you participate in graduate school. Although these questions may be personal to us, we also believe that some of these same questions will become "graduate school lore language." Hence, by addressing the questions in each chapter, we hope to assist graduate students in understanding the processes of graduate school via long distance.

Although our writing style is not "chatty," it is informal and practical. Potential graduate students like you need something that is "light" to read. In all graduate programs, students will have the opportunity to read formalized pieces of research written in a highly scientific format. Most of our research is anecdotal and comes from our experiences, our cohorts' experiences, and e-mail sent us via a distance learning listserv. It is through the words of these people—and our words—that you will receive information, and thus a formal approach isn't appropriate.

One caveat in reading this book: The moment we write something about long distance learning or talk about a particular university or a specific technology, it will change. In fact, by the time you pick up this book, some of the information may be out of date—and we will probably be in motion updating the data. Distance education is too mobile and ever-changing. Hence, you must remember that this book is really a rough draft that could be rewritten every single month, probably every single day. We doubt if we could keep up that pace, however.

Remember what our experiences have been, because we suspect you might have the opportunity to experience similar ones. We want to enlighten you and give you some real facts from real graduate students who have been there, done that, got the degree, and lived happily ever after—or at least purported to live happily ever after. Consider this as an expository of our trek and the trek of others who are included through graduate school. We are just thankful for the opportunity to have participated in a long distance learning program. We hope you have a good time. Good luck!

ACKNOWLEDGMENTS

In writing a subjective book such as this one, we find we need to thank a host of people. First, a huge thank you to the graduate students who participated in the survey and expressed candidly their feelings about attending and graduating from long distance graduate programs. Second, a round of applause to the professors and trainers in long distance education programs who shared their experiences and enlightened us from a different perspective. Third, thanks to our work colleagues and to the custodians who left the lights on when they left at nights. Fourth, huge thanks to Dr. Bruce Thyer from the University of Georgia. His numerous pages of judicious commentary on our manuscript were extremely beneficial to us. Fifth, the most important thanks go to our wives Joanne (Darrel) and Margaret (Steve) and our children Anna Rose and Hailey (Darrel) and Jennifer, Mark, and Meghan (Steve).

It was a rewarding experience!

DARREL L. HAMMON, PhD,
dhammon@lcsc.edu
STEVEN K. ALBISTON, PhD,
steve_a@admin.eitc.edu

1

AN INTRODUCTION

So you want to find and complete a graduate program via long distance? As you begin to search for an appropriate long distance graduate program, understand that completing a graduate program long distance is not the same as being on campus. We are qualified to write this book because we have gone through every stage of completing a doctoral program via long distance. From writing the letter that initiated the program in eastern Idaho, to taking classes in four different cities, to designing specific courses, to taking preliminary examinations ("prelims") with our cohort group, to actually graduating, we have completed the cycle. In this book we take what were unknowns to us and pair them with our hard-earned experience to offer a clear view of long distance learning—from those who have gone through the experience and lived to tell about it.

With the increased impact of technology in our lives, particularly on-line and televised courses, education as we know it has dramatically changed the way most institutions of higher learning look at educating their students. Moreover, these changes will likely continue at an accelerating rate. This technological philosophy of education emphasizes not what the university or college wants but rather what the diverse population of adult learners needs. In addition, the method of delivery has emerged as an important ingredient in education circles. When it comes to enrolling in graduate programs, or any educational program, you want to ask a series of simple questions. Because of technology and the long distance capability,

* Why do I need to be on campus to complete my courses?
* Why do I have to quit working in order to enroll in a full-time program?
* Aren't there night or on-line courses for me?
* Can't the graduate program come to me instead of me going to it?

We asked the same questions of officials at one major university and received a favorable response: "We can accommodate those needs if you are willing to sacrifice time, energy, and endure a varied schedule." In time, we both received our PhDs from the University of Idaho while living in Idaho Falls, more than 500 miles from the main campus in Moscow, Idaho. Our professors traveled to Idaho Falls from the Boise Center campus of the University and from the main campus in Moscow. Because of these traveling professors, we were able to complete most of our course work in Idaho Falls, supplementing our program with various courses from Idaho State University (ISU) in Pocatello, 50 miles south of Idaho Falls. We completed our university's residency requirement and preliminary examinations at the Boise Center, 250 miles from the main campus in Idaho Falls. Most of our doctoral research was completed by using libraries at ISU, Ricks College (a private, church-owned college 24 miles north of Idaho Falls), through interlibrary loan, and by sharing materials with colleagues around the United States who were completing similar programs of study. Darrel stepped onto the University of Idaho's main campus in Moscow for the first time on the day he graduated. Steve, however, had earned his master's degree from the U of I. But neither one of us went to the main campus at all during our doctoral program!

Once we finished our doctoral program, though, we knew we were not finished with the education process. We are both lifelong (perpetual) learners and continue doing educational things such as presenting workshops, working on staff development programs, serving on state and regional committees as officers and participating members, and providing leadership at our college. So we thought, "Why not write a book about what had just happened to us?" We were sure that many other similarly situated potential graduate students would wonder if long distance graduate school could be done. Our sole reason for writing this book is to share our experiences and the experiences of others enrolling in and finally completing a graduate program via long distance.

We knew that other potential graduate students might be contemplating the same long distance or on-line route to learning, and we believed others might benefit from the collective wisdom of a variety of graduate students from across the United States and abroad.

We had several goals in writing this book, including,

- Helping students identify long distance graduate schools
- Informing graduate students of the various stages of graduate school matriculation
- Providing information to graduates about how to establish long distance rapport and professional relationships with graduate faculty and staff
- Providing students with specific help in negotiating with their workplaces, families, and extracurricular activities
- Helping students become acquainted with working with cohort groups in their service area
- Providing students with information on how they can interview and select graduate committees via long distance
- Providing students with information about how our cohort group developed programs of study, completed preliminary exams, and completed a thesis or dissertation—all via long distance
- Discussing the technological methods of doing literature reviews

In order to help us answer our questions and, we hope, yours, we informally surveyed a variety of different people across the United States, Canada, England, Wales, and Jamaica. We sent a survey to many of our Idaho colleagues. We also subscribed to a listserv, provided to the distance education community by the American Center for the Study of Distance Education (DEOS-L Listserv). You can subscribe to this listserv by contacting them at DEOS-L@PSUVM.PSU.EDU. Over time, we collected responses from fellow distance learners about their experiences, and these are described throughout the book. The survey itself is more fully explained in Chapter 2.

With the advent of distance education available over telephone lines, a new world of learning opportunities has been created for both rural and metropolitan Americans. What had been limited to those who could travel long distances and be absent from work became more readily available to those homebound, employed full-time, or occupied as parents.

If we pontificate a bit about completing graduate degrees via distance education, please forgive us. We live in a different world from those who are close to university and college campuses. Like many of the survey respondents, we work full-time and have families. We both are highly involved in community and religious activities, and we live in a wonderful community close to the Tetons, Yellowstone Park, and the greatest snow on earth, and we enjoy other amenities such as low crime and very little traffic. Our lives are full, as are yours. Do you blame us for not wanting to quit our jobs or travel extensively to the big city and take courses? If you are contemplating completing a graduate program long distance, this is the book for you. Because this book is more emotive than theoretical, you might decide to enroll or not enroll, depending on what you read and feel during the next few pages. We will expose the pros and cons and let you be the judge. Although we will show you both the good and the bad sides to long distance education graduate programs, we can safely say long distance education was the most appropriate educational delivery model for us. For you—well, that's something for you to decide after you read the following information, contemplate why you really want a graduate degree, and what price—mental, emotional, financial—you want to pay for the honor of being a graduate student and earning a master's or doctoral degree. We also suggest that you write to and visit with others who have participated in such programs as you travel around to different staff development activities and explore various listservs that discuss distance education. It is important for you to do your homework early, because once you commit to a long distance learning program, you will want to finish and be successful.

Good luck! We are available to discuss our decision to complete a program via long distance, and we welcome your suggestions on this topic. Our e-mail and snail mail addresses and telephone numbers are at the end of Chapter 11. Because completing graduate school via long distance is still evolving, we hope that you will share with us your experiences, positive or negative. Others need to know that they are not the only ones "swimming in the froth of graduate school."

GLOSSARY

We will be using a variety of terms, perhaps new to the graduate student. If you already know them, please disregard the following information. If you do not know them yet, then review them before you plow through the rest of the chapters. We have tried to define these terms as we use them in this book. Understandably, there are probably better or more accurate definitions, but these are ones we understand and hope you understand, too. If not, ask a computer guru where you go to school or work to explain the technical terms.

Bookmarking A method of electronically saving your place on the Internet for future reference.

Browser A type of Internet search engine that allows you to explore various topics. Some browsers include Netscape and Microsoft Explorer.

Chatting A form of communication via the Internet using chatting software.

Cohort Group The group of students who enroll in the same distance education program you do. They become, in essence, your surrogate family until you finish your program. Your cohort group can play a key role in motivating you to stay in the program, completing tasks as assigned, and helping with travel costs.

DEOS-L Listserv A service provided to the Distance Education community by the American Center for the Study of Distance Education, the Pennsylvania State University.

Distance Learning The concept of learning anything via Internet, outreach sites, and so forth.

E-mail The electronic transmission of text.

Internet The electronic information highway.

Long Distance Education Completing any educational activity at a distance from the originated site.

Listservs Discussion groups that interact via the Internet.

On-line A term used to show that a class comes via the Internet.

Snail Mail Using the United States Post Office. Because of the advent of e-mail, the use of the Post Office has come to be known as "snail mail."

URL Universal Resource Location.

WWW The World Wide Web (or the WEB).

2

An Overview of Long Distance Learning Graduate Programs

Technology is nothing more or less than a natural phase of the creative process which engaged man from the moment he forged his first tool and began to transform the world of its humanization.

—Pablo Friere in Cultural Action for Freedom.
From a signature on an e-mail from
Martin Owen, Project REM Director,
University of Wales, Bangor, July 23, 1996

The proliferation of computers coming on-line for a multitude of reasons, especially educational, and the inclusion of telecommunications at most colleges and universities constitute reasons enough for a review of "doing graduate school" without leaving the workplace or hometown for extended periods of time. More and more colleges and universities are rethinking their educational delivery systems. Even small technical colleges such as Eastern Idaho Technical College in

Idaho Falls, Idaho—our hometown—have written and received long distance learning grants from federal and state agencies to develop downlink sites to deliver technical education to rural sites. Most of the academic 4-year institutions in Idaho have also applied for and received similar grants. Within a short time, we will all be connected together and be able to deliver courses to each other. These communities and colleges receive such grants under the auspices of "economic development" and outreach delivery of educational services. As a consequence, other universities and colleges are seeking creative ways to increase their involvement in the economic development in their communities. What better way than to collaborate with business, industry, and education? Hence, the discovery of education as an economic boon within an educational region has become an integral part of many communities' economic development strategic plans.

In addition, administrators, teachers, and both high school and postsecondary students, especially in rural settings, seek other learning sources. Funding for education has a propensity to shrink when we most need it. Many high schools do not have certified teachers in specialized areas. But if one school has a teacher who can teach astronomy, for example, then the rest of the rural schools can share that valuable resource.

Another population benefits also. The adults who are enmeshed in their communities and have growing families or have family ties in the area in which they live are not always willing to drive more than 160 miles one way, especially in severe winter conditions, to receive education. They demand that education "come to them." Institutions who fail to attempt to deliver educational services to their "customers" will soon see—if they have not already—enrollment decreases that quickly can spell financial doom. Hence, it is imperative that higher education institutions reevaluate their delivery methods.

Many colleges and universities are recognizing the need to add alternate delivery methods and provide education services via distance learning. The resources change rapidly, but for a start you can access information on the Internet through the DEOS-L Listserv (Appendix 1) or you can check out the list of colleges and universities at the Globewide Network Academy homepage, http://www.gnacademy.org/ (Appendix 2).

Students are becoming older, wiser, and more conscientious about their time demands and the availability of receiving classes via video, high-tech peripherals, and on-line computer services; therefore, potential graduate students need to be aware of "doing education" long distance. Although receiving classes via computer or participating in higher education through distance learning or outreach centers may seem to be a partial panacea to their educational needs, graduate students need to be aware of the pros and cons of completing a degree in such a technological fashion. Many potential graduate students who think that staying home and completing their education via long distance is the ultimate in true adult education simultaneously need to understand that their personal responsibility drastically increases and their connection, both personal and technological, to the university becomes more important.

VARIOUS FORMS OF EDUCATIONAL TECHNOLOGY

Distance learning can take the guise of various forms of educational technology. We want to review some of the most common, although you must understand that over time, other forms will rise out of the technological craze of the 1990s that we cannot yet imagine. Nevertheless, you should be aware of some of the current forms.

The first is the one with which we are the most familiar—off-campus classes, offered live with real professors who talk and stand in front of the class. Because of the clamor from people off campus, many universities and colleges are encouraging their undergraduate and graduate programs to leave the confines of campus and travel to the hinterlands. Some professors balk at this, but when they begin to see their class loads dwindle and their sections disappear because of the requests off campus, they soon appreciate the concept.

Having real professors in off-campus classes is both good and bad. First the bad: Because they are required to leave the comfortable confines of their own classrooms and travel to unfamiliar territory where the comforts of home may be scarce, some may be reluctant instructors and exude some sort of negativism. However, we have discovered that once they see how motivated off-campus students are, they are usually quick to change their attitudes and feelings. Many such professors with whom we have visited have told us about their outreach students. Often they become their hardest working graduate students. Also, these professors become some of the best instructors in the classroom. Not confined to the rigors of the campus, they soon become more at ease visiting with students. However, although they are more prone to visit with students, they have limited time in the outreach area to converse with or counsel students. More often than not, they come to town to teach and then head back to the university. We suggest that in this situation, you and your class sit down with the professor and schedule specific times for him or her to visit with you. Most will set specific office hours in the outreach area.

Another form of education technology are the off-campus classes offered via interactive television, with professors in the "home studio." This form also has its pros and cons. For those who love to have a professor in the classroom at all times, off-campus classes via television are not for them. Professors who use this mode of delivery may never actually visit these classrooms other than through television. Often when you want to converse or ask a question, you have to push a button in front of you and speak. Sometimes the technology actually breaks down—often this becomes the norm not the exception. In such cases, your class will probably be canceled—or you may just see your professor and not hear him or her or just the opposite. In some of the more advanced technology, especially if it is not tuned just right, you will hear screeching—and it does not come from the professor scratching his or her nails on the black/white board. However, this particular medium is quickly becoming the standard by which colleges and universities are delivering their off-campus classes.

A third form of educational technology has been around for some time, although some of the methods have been upgraded. This form is independent study programs that offer individual courses or entire programs. Independent study programs are for those, in our opinions, who are self-directed learners, those who are motivated to do the work without prodding from a professor or going to class two or three or even four times per week. In independent study programs you enroll in programs as does any other student. You are assigned a professor who sends you the course material via videotapes, audiotapes, regular books, and assignments. Then you have to take the initiative, complete the assignments, take the tests, send in the material, receive the feedback, and—it is hoped—complete the course or program. You and the professor communicate through any of the electronic media: telephone, e-mail, fax, and so forth. Again, this type of program can be wonderful if, as we said earlier, you are a self-directed, motivated learner. If you are the type who needs a daily routine of going to class, plopping down in a hard seat, listening to lectures, taking tests when scheduled, and doing whatever else you do in a regular class, then the independent study programs are definitely not for you.

Still another form of educational technology is the computer-assisted instruction offered via e-mail or the World Wide Web (WWW). Although this is one of the newest forms of instruction, it is fast becoming one of the most prolific. It seems every institution, whether accredited or not, is gearing up for the rush. Even high school students can obtain a high school diploma using this method of study. Again, you have to be cautious about what type of graduate program is being offered through the WWW. Do your homework before you actually enroll and pay big money for a course. Just as you have to be cautious about some telephone solicitors, so too you have to be doubly cautious about "colleges" offering courses via the computer. You cannot talk to them in person, and the Better Business Bureau in your area probably has not had time to review any of these sources.

However, many reputable institutions of higher learning have developed their own on-line courses and offer them through their homepage. If you know the institution and its reputation, then their computer-assisted programs have probably had to go through the same scrutiny and process for course or program approval. For example, at our institution, faculty members must go through a particular process to change or alter a current course or program or develop a new course or program. These procedures ensure the course or program has gone through the appropriate channels before it goes "on air."

One of the positive features of instruction on-line is the communication capabilities some of these courses have. For example, two courses Darrel has been working on—government and citizenship—have great capability. Students are able to converse through e-mail. The instructor can post assignments and announcements to the bulletin board for all the students enrolled in class. If students have questions about a particular part of the assignment, they can immediately e-mail their instructor or a member of their class. Often, the reply is immediate. We have discovered students like to chat using e-mail. (Of course, some students do not watch their spelling, grammar, punctuation, and sentence structure.)

In addition, parts of the curriculum have links to other Web pages or sites that enhance the lesson. Being able to participate in on-line courses allows the classroom, as we have previously known it, to expand beyond anything that has ever been developed. However, often you have to remind yourself of the time frames with which you are working and have to come back to the assignment at hand. It is easy to go "cruising" on the WWW for a couple of hours and then not know where the time has gone.

Finally—although probably not the last form to be used as educational technology—is attending regular classes on campus part-time while commuting from another city. Like the other forms, this has both negative and positive aspects. Having to drive to the campus can be the biggest drawback. For example, we live more than 50 miles one way from Idaho State University. Some of you may laugh at a "mere" 50 miles, but if you have ever been to Idaho in the winter and seen blowing and drifting snow, you will soon stop laughing. Driving in terrible weather is truly a deterrent to taking classes away from home. Besides, many of the courses are either taught at night or during the day when you are working. Being away from home for a 3-hour course with an additional 2 hours of driving time is a terrible way to pick up three credits.

However, being on campus has its positive aspects. One of the most important to us is being close to the library. Living away from campus and trying to do research are difficult. Of course, you have to plan for time to be at the library, either driving down on Saturday or taking additional time off work or time away from the family to accomplish this task. Usually, you do not become as attached to campus life as you perhaps were as an undergraduate student. Often you drive to class, listen for your 3-hour block, and then head back home to your other responsibilities. This is one of the many reasons some colleges and universities are trying to bring the campus to the students.

Overall, any of various forms of educational technology by which distance learning can take place can be helpful in obtaining a graduate degree. Often, some, if not all, of these may be offered by your institution. Also, some graduate programs offer a mix of various educational technologies. Again, it requires some sleuthing to see what your graduate program offers. We strongly suggest that you do the appropriate research on any of the programs, or any other technologies that will be available to you in the coming years, and go forward. Do not wait. As we say to our students, "Sometimes you have to go out on a limb to really see the whole tree." The bottom line is this: Be creative, innovative, and technologically motivated. There are so many new and innovative ways to do education. Find one that suits you the best. A good source for you to review is *The Electronic*

University Guidebook. Peruse it and ask a ton of questions. You will not be disappointed.

SURVEY RESPONDENTS

Much of the information that we have included in this book comes from various graduate students who were willing to participate in our study. All respondents were volunteers. They chose to participate. We mailed surveys to our cohort group, to other University of Idaho and Idaho State University graduate students. (If you wish to obtain a copy of the survey, please e-mail either one of us, and we will send you a copy.) We also posted a letter on the distance learning listserv and requested that those who participated in a graduate program via long distance respond. We sent the respondents a survey via e-mail or snail mail. As a consequence, some of the information propounded in this book may seem biased. All in all, they are honest words from real graduate students who participated in a long distance graduate program. Most graduated from these programs; others, we discovered, are still "long distancing it"; still others dropped out of the program.

Please understand that our methods of collecting the data were not intended to follow the rigors of a scientific study. We chose to collect information from a select group and informally report our findings in narrative form coupled with data tables. What we have discovered leads us to believe that there are a number of scientific studies that could be conducted in this area. Many of the questions for further study will be addressed in our summary chapter.

Types of Degrees Earned

The respondents to our survey were in pursuit of various graduate degrees. Results indicated that 24% of the respondents were enrolled in either PhD or EdD programs. The remaining 76% were enrolled in MA, MS, MBA, or MEd programs. More than 70% of the respondents were women.

Respondents' Colleges

It was extremely interesting to learn where the survey respondents attended colleges and universities. The institutions demonstrate the wide variety of graduate programs available through some form of distance learning. The colleges and universities represented are

* Albertson College (Idaho)
* Idaho State University (Idaho)
* Montana State University (Montana)
* New School for Social Research (New York)
* Portland State University (Oregon)
* Sonoma State University (California)
* St. Francis Xavier Antigomish (Nova Scotia, Canada)
* University of Arizona (Arizona)
* University of Idaho (Idaho)
* University of Phoenix (Arizona)
* University of Washington (Washington)
* University of Wyoming (Wyoming)

POINTS TO REMEMBER

* The options available to students who choose to participate in distance learning programs are increasing at a rapid rate.
* A good listserv for distance learning is DEOS-L Listserv.
* The scope of our survey was limited to our cohort group and a few others who were contacted through a distance learning listserv. Therefore, we cannot assume that the material gathered can be generalized to the total population of distance learners.
* A copy of our survey can be obtained by e-mailing either of us.
* There are various forms of educational technology by which distance learning can take place. Many colleges and universities offer a mix of these.

3

IDENTIFYING AN
APPROPRIATE INSTITUTION

In a few years [distance learning] will be considered going to a campus and knowledge locally will be the expected norm—like the printing press, the electronic world will force traditional campuses to reorganize themselves and try to understand why someone should be on a campus for a [distance learning] experience.

—An e-mail from Tom Abeles, July 22, 1996

One of the keys to selecting a graduate school is determining your needs as a potential graduate student. This chapter focuses on identifying an appropriate institution for the graduate student. Prior to choosing an appropriate long distance graduate school, you must eventually ask yourself several questions:

* Why do I really want to complete a graduate (or even undergraduate) degree long distance?
* What type of graduate degree do I want?
* Is the degree program reputable and accredited?

* Does the university/college in my community/state/region have distance learning courses offered in my community or within a reasonable traveling distance?
* When are the courses taught?
* Will there be a scope and sequence to the courses?
* What if I miss a particular sequence of courses during a specific semester?
* Will the sequence of courses be offered again within a reasonable amount of time?
* Will I have a cohort group available to me?
* If the courses are on-line, is there local Internet access or do I need to dial a long distance Internet access provider?
* What type of residency requirements might there be?
* To whom do I write my letter so the university will deliver courses and a graduate program here?
* Where do I obtain books?
* Who is the contact person at the local community college or high school?
* Will I remain working full-time?
* Do I want to travel?
* Do I *need* to travel?
* How much time do I have to devote to this program of study?
* Will the program allow me to participate full- or part-time?
* What methods or modes of delivery does the institution have to offer?
* What are the costs if it is an out-of-state institution?
* What technology peripherals will I need in order to make a connection to the university?
* Will the local high school, community, or technical college allow transmission of satellite/telecommunication broadcasts?

By far, this list of questions is not exhaustive, and we do not mean it to be. These are a few questions that we asked ourselves before we enrolled in our long distance doctoral program. What we tried to do is ask the same questions of those who received the survey. We wanted to know from them, especially because they represented all parts of the United States, Canada, and other parts of the world, what types of questions they were asking themselves and what answers they expected—and what answers they actually received.

21st Century College Apparel

For the most part respondents wanted an institution close to their homes, primarily because of family and jobs. Many of us did not want to have to quit our jobs or be away from our families for long periods of time. We also, like many of our colleagues, did not want to travel long distances each week to complete our graduate programs. However, sometimes what we want and what is available are two distinct items.

Typically, the number of miles from respondents' homes to the graduate school was more than 40 miles. More than 46% of all respondents said they lived more than 200 miles from their graduate school. All doctoral students were more than 200 miles from their graduate school. Distance did play a significant role in our program. Of course, having classes offered in our hometown was wonderful, although we had to spend summers in Boise as part of our residency requirement. But the residency requirements in some programs are changing. We suspect that as time goes on, many distance graduate programs will review their residency requirements and make reasonable accommodations for their students.

We began our program prior to the inception of on-line courses. As a result, our options were limited to the types of courses compared to those available in today's long distance market. Our primary reason for choosing the University of Idaho was cost and distance—the college where we work has an articulation agreement with Idaho's institutions of higher learning that offers university and college employees a dynamite deal.

A master's student said he opted for his MBA program from Idaho State University (ISU) because it was the only business program ISU offered in Idaho Falls. His response was typical of those we surveyed. Because they lived and worked in one community, it was difficult to pull up stakes and move to a community where a graduate university was located. Often we talk about people's flexibility, but when you really think about it most of us who have worked full-time at fairly good jobs for a moderate length of time are tied to the community because of family, friends, church, and recreational opportunities, and it is nigh impossible to leave. Most of us have been out of the going-to-school routine long enough that being poor again—or still, in some cases—did not evoke any nostalgic feelings.

Although many of our respondents stated the only reason why they completed their program was because they were "land-locked" and could not get away, distance graduate programs are becoming more prolific and available. Now with the numerous "external degree" programs being offered via long distance, graduate students across the world have a variety of programs from which to choose. They do not have to pick the closest one to their home. It may take some time and effort, but potential graduate students can research the best program for them. With the research capabilities and the common telephone, students have greater access to information than ever before.

Although some undergraduate and graduate students spend a great deal of time and energy in searching out their ideal program of study, some universities and colleges are actively seeking students. They understand the importance of marketing their programs. In our survey, for example, one doctoral student wrote that two of the professors from his graduate program visited his worksite to discuss the doctoral program with interested individuals. Because of the initiative of the professors from the university and their excitement about the potential of the program, he signed up immediately. Had they not come to his worksite, chances are he probably would not have taken the initiative to enroll.

Other comments that were shared follow.

* "I chose my program based on the convenience in achieving the degree!"
* "Having previously attended an on-campus program far from home, I needed to go where I could be at home and work."
* "A combination of the college having the program that I desired, it was the closest to my home and offered the intensity that I expected."
* "By considering proximity to my job; program that I was interested in; and traffic flows."
* "I researched for an institution that had the specialty that I desired."

ACCREDITATION

We believe it is extremely important to find a graduate school—or any school for that matter—that is appropriately accredited. If you are reviewing a college or university graduate bulletin, you will want to look for a statement much like this one: "The University of Idaho is a member of the National Association of State Universities and Land-Grant Colleges and is accredited by the Northwest Association of Schools and Colleges." An appropriate accreditation by the proper accrediting entity is probably one of the most important criteria by which to judge a graduate school. To review university or college accreditation, refer to a variety of publications such as the National Center for Educational Statistics, *Directory of Postsecondary Institutions*, *Higher Education Directory,* or *Peterson's Guide to Distance Learning.* However, in some of these publications, colleges self-report accreditation and are not necessarily verified by publishers. You should take the initiative and call accrediting entities and verify accreditation.

In the United States, the Commission on Recognition of Postsecondary Accreditation (CORPA, formerly COPA) is a private agency responsible for accreditation matters. CORPA is a seven-member body that has representation from individuals with interests of public, specialized, institutional, and regional accrediting agencies, and of organizations representing colleges, universities, and governing bodies. CORPA reviews accreditation policies, procedures, and administration. Regional accrediting agencies review the process for accredited colleges and universities.

For example, currently our institution is going through our 10-year accreditation process. For more than one year, we have been preparing an accreditation review—it's more of a book, actually—that documents all facets of our institution. Then, our accrediting entity, a panel of several educators representing Northwest Accrediting Association, comes to our institution and spends several days reviewing the document, visiting with faculty and staff, and reviewing other records that are pertinent for our accreditation process. When they have finished their review, they will signify by mail and certificate that we are accredited. The accreditation process is lengthy, and the team from Northwest will not leave any stone or textbook unturned.

Unfortunately, this type of review is not completed at some institutions of higher learning that profess to be "accredited." It is your job to use your jaundiced eye when reviewing the credentials of each institution. As Dr. Bruce Thyer of the University of Georgia aptly stated in a letter (September 24, 1996) to us, "Students simply *must* ensure that the institution is suitably accredited, in order for their degree to have any merit."

Because everyone seems to want a graduate degree, and some institutions want to accommodate this love of degrees, there has emerged from the bogs of educational accommodation a new breed of institutions. These institutions offer master's and doctorate degrees for a price, for doing very little work, or for verifying you have had life experiences. Reputable institutions and educators have aptly labeled these schools "diploma mills." A good source to review regarding diploma mills and how they operate is Stewart and Spille's (1988) *Diploma Mills: Degrees by Fraud.* The book was published by the American Council on Education, a judicious reviewer of educational activities in the United States.

According to Stewart and Spille, anyone can form a corporation and call itself an accredited institution. A corporation can say it is accredited and write its accreditation dialog in its catalogs. But this is definitely no substitute for the important and "precious imprimatur" of the Council on Postsecondary Education or its regional affiliates. One particular institution, considered a diploma mill, offers a doctorate for $295, payable by credit card. According to Dr. Thyer, "Quite literally legally nothing prevents one from paying these fees, getting the certificate, and appending PhD after one's name on one's résumé." However, there can be no substitutes for a proper credential from an appropriately accredited institution.

In some colleges and universities, graduate degree programs are subject to separate accreditation processes, although the entire college has received its own accreditation. For example, the American Psychological Association accredits doctoral programs in clinical, counseling, and school psychology. You should be aware when making inquiries into graduate programs of their accreditation status. Perhaps one of the most important questions you could ask is, "Is this program accredited by a relevant professional association (Do you know the professional association you need to have)?" Often, job opportunities state candidates must have received their graduate degree from an institution that has been accredited by a particular professional association. If you do not abide by these standards, you may have a difficult time securing a job in your chosen market.

Dr. Thyer commented that he knew a young man who was completing his JD degree through an institution in a particular state via videotape. The irony is that when he finishes his degree, he will be eligible to take the bar in that state, but his JD degree will not be recognized to take the bar or even practice in other states. Surely, this should propel graduate students to review the consequences of a degree from a particular institution. The old adage, "buyer beware" (a.k.a. "Graduate students, beware of improperly accredited institutions") is still sound advice.

TECHNOLOGY PERIPHERALS USED

We felt that the use of instructional technology would play an important role in the success of students participating in long distance graduate programs. However, responses regarding using technology peripherals was probably the most surprising. Many of the comments were along the lines of, "More use of technology could improve [X graduate program]." However, these graduate students used a variety of technology, including computers, CD-ROMS, on-line searches, on-line chats, e-mail, on-line classes, scanners, fax machines, and satellites. Most graduate students used a computer during their course work, although some did not (about 33% of the EdD and MEd students did not). Although the majority of respondents used on-line searches, e-mail, and faxes, very few used the new on-line chat software. The reason probably hinges on the newness of the technology. Respondents also reported little or no use of satellites in their programs. If we were to give the same survey to graduate students 4 to 6 years from now, we believe that the majority of the respondents would say they used chatting software and satellite communication as integral tools for communication and courses during graduate school via long distance.

The use of peripherals in conducting research and completing projects during the course of enrollment during a graduate program varied widely. Some of the variance was a result in part to the level of comfort felt by the student. Some was a function of access. In our case, we have had the good fortune of working at a technical college that has the latest technology readily available to all faculty and staff. In addition, we are expected to use this technology rather than try to muddle through with archaic methods. Some respondents were not so lucky. Either they were located in a small community so far removed that it was difficult to gain access to the tools that were on the market or their program of study did not require or teach to technology.

Our doctoral program was a bit of a contradiction. On one hand, we studied the latest versions of statistical software that we could use to crunch our numbers, and we spent hours with library staff members learning how to use the latest on-line search drivers. Yet when it came time to sit for the preliminary examination, we drove approximately 250 miles to respond to questions by writing in blue books with pens and pencils! Steve commented, "Why didn't we just use monks as scribes?" It appears to us that if we are to move yet further into the mode of distance education, we ought to use all of the technology that is available to its fullest extent.

POINTS TO REMEMBER

* Make certain that you consider your needs during the process of selecting a graduate program.
* Understand the impact of travel time. (It is hoped that by the time this book is published, this should be less of an issue because of ever-increasing technology that will make physical transportation unnecessary.)
* Ask about residency requirements—not state of residence but rather the number of credits one must take on the campus or at an approved off-campus site to fulfill graduation requirements.

THE APPLICATION PROCESS

*I don't remember the details [of the application process]
but I do remember doing it via phone and mail and it was
really a hassle. When I got to the campus, they couldn't
find my file and did not know who had it.*

—MA graduate student

Part of the application process includes understanding that all or part
of it will be done long distance, although some programs will enroll
you on the first day of class. As a consequence, it is imperative to
establish immediate rapport with the graduate school staff. It is
desirable to find a contact person who will take a special interest in
you and follow up when you have specific questions about any part
of the application process. Some of the questions that you may be
asking include,

* How long will the application process take?
* What is the best method of delivering documents to the graduate
  school—fax, e-mail, an overnight mail service, regular mail (snail
  mail), courier?

* How do I maintain constant communication with the graduate school?
* What are the fees?
* Do I have a copy of the most current publication of the graduate catalog with all the rules, regulations, and guidelines?
* What are the requirements of the application process? Who is responsible for what? What are the deadlines? To whom do I pay my fees?
* What assessments are necessary for me? Where can I take the GRE, MAT, GMAT, LSAT, or other graduate assessment?
* What about letters of reference?
* If there is an interview process, can I do it via telecommunications?

GENERAL APPLICATION PROCEDURES

For graduate programs, the application process may resemble the intensity of our undergraduate programs. Part of the process includes an application form, an application fee, the appropriate graduate test, letters of recommendation, a philosophy paper, a summary of your life, and other documents, depending on the institution. Normally, most of the documents need to be sent together as a packet. The letters of recommendation are usually sent separately. Be sure, however, to individually contact your references. Sometimes, they need some follow up to remind them of the due dates.

For us, it was mind boggling to think about how the application process worked long distance. Although we were not on campus, we had a graduate catalog and tried to follow the sequence of events. Steve had no problem because he had done his undergraduate and master's program at the U of I, and they already had his file. Darrel was a different story. His application process was long, grueling, and somewhat frustrating. The first batch of information he sent to the graduate school at the U of I was lost somewhere between his home and the graduate school. Although he still enrolled in courses, he was not admitted to the graduate program for almost a year. He discovered that it was imperative to call the graduate school frequently to see what had arrived and what had not. Keeping on top of the application process should become your priority once you send in your application and fee.

One graduate student wrote that she had not been accepted in the program and wondered why. She called 6 months after sending in the application and her portion of the paperwork only to find out she was missing one of the three letters of reference. Everything else that had arrived was safely in her folder. Another doctoral student stated, "My application process was a little rough. Two files were made on me. One was complete and the other incomplete. This took a while to discover along with many phone calls."

Most graduate schools will not process your application until all of your "stuff" has been checked off. Sometimes, however, you can convince the dean of the graduate school to forward your application on for approval even though you lack one letter. A doctoral student gave us a bit of advice about the application process:

> We could have used e-mail technology to expedite the process. Also, I observed other applicants having difficulty moving through the application process. It seemed like materials would get lost and that long periods of time would go by before getting a response from the office dealing with the applications. Again, this would be more efficient if the university would establish a homepage that included all of the necessary forms so that an applicant could complete the process "on-line."

However, most student had few if any problems in the application process. Many of them responded that their professors or major advisors were the most influential in helping them matriculate. Some said they returned to their undergraduate programs, and fortunately, the registrar still had their file. As one MBA respondent said, "It was very simple. An application, a transcript, the G-MAT, and I was in." If only all of us had such a simple process.

Perhaps the ease with which one can become matriculated is a function of the length of time an institution has been in the business of serving students at a distance. Some would say that we might be too kind with this statement and that any student's application should receive the same treatment, regardless of his or her proximity to campus. The fact is that it is much easier to "drop by" the dean's office before or after class to check on the status of your application than it is to converse long distance. There is something to be said about the value of face-to-face dialogue.

STUDENT OPINIONS OF
THE APPLICATION PROCESS

The following is a representative list of responses to the survey question, "What was your application process like?"

* "Lengthy!"
* "An application packet was sent to me through the mail. I was required to complete and submit to the university application papers as well as transcripts from all previous colleges attended, letters of recommendation, and extensive written responses to some questions."
* "Fairly straight forward. They had openings in their program. I picked up an application packet, talked with the program coordinator and was given a shot."
* "No problem. The outreach office made the process simple."
* "It took a while to know if I was accepted (3–5 months)."
* "The application process was easy but the wait was tedious."
* "I knew that the process could be confusing, so I developed a time line for me to check in with the graduate school to see what had been received and what was still needed."
* "It was long and not well organized. The requirements were fine but materials were often lost. Technology improvements are needed!"

We recommend that you become extremely familiar with the application process. If possible, a trip to the campus for personal introductions could help to establish a relationship with the stewards of the application materials. You will discover what appropriate forms are needed, if a graduate test is required, and if any interviews are necessary. Remember it is just as important for you to seek information as it is for your graduate school to provide it.

You will process a mound of paperwork from the time you first enroll until you have received your diploma. Organization and documentation are two other key ingredients to your success. Start a file and keep copies of everything that you submit. We recommend that you date each item completed in your files.

POINTS TO REMEMBER

* Take the time to become fully aware of the application requirements before you embark on your graduate school experience.
* Make a connection with someone in the office who handles the application paperwork, such as the office secretary. If possible have several conversations with this person so that you are remembered.
* Do not assume that everything is going well just because you have not heard anything to the contrary. We have discovered that "no news" can really mean "bad news." Make sure that you follow up on your application materials.
* Develop a time line that prompts you to follow up on the application process until you have completed all of the steps.
* Keep a file that contains copies of everything that you do from the time that you first seek admission information until you have received your diploma.

5

ARRANGING YOUR LIFE
AND NEGOTIATING TIME

*This is the most difficult part of this type of program, and
I continue to struggle with prioritizing study time around
my children's activities. It is very easy for me to put off
studying! I have found, however, it is much easier and
less distractive to study at the library than at home.*

—Graduate, City College, Renton, Washington

Part of determining whether or not a long distance graduate school is
an appropriate method for you to obtain a degree involves determining how the experience will impact your life. Scheduling your time is
important, maybe the most important facet in deciding whether to go
to graduate school. Graduate school is never a picnic. And graduate
school via long distance offers new challenges.

Some of the questions to contemplate as you read this chapter are,

* How much time is this really going to take?
* How will I negotiate time with my family, friends, employment?

* What sacrifices am I going to have to make?
* Is this program a continuous program, semester after semester, including summers?
* Am I really willing to make the sacrifice of money and time to do a distance learning program?
* Do I realize that sometimes travel of long distances may be involved?
* Do I understand that developing the courses may be my responsibility?
* Am I willing to schedule my own classes?
* Am I willing to work with local businesses and community colleges to negotiate time to use their facilities if I do not have the technological peripherals?
* How can I include my family in this process?

Probably one of the most important questions you must ask yourself is this: "What type of time negotiation must I make along the way." For us, we had to negotiate time at every level. Almost 80% of all respondents were married and had families. All students except one in our cohort group were married and had children.

Granted, those who attend or return to graduate school are typically more mature and have established themselves in the business world. For most graduate students, families become the premier ingredient in selecting, attending, and completing graduate school. Although students who are on campus and participating in campus life in specific blocks of time find that their schedules change somewhat, completing a degree long distance requires a completely different approach. In most cases, the university is hundreds of miles away. Students do not have instant access to professors or libraries. Arranging your life and negotiating time become important cogs to fit into the wheel of life. In addition, if graduate students decide to remain working full-time, there will be instances in which they must negotiate time with their employer in order to attend class. Some employers have "administrative leave." Other employers require students to take time off without pay. Time away from work can and has been an issue in the past in that residency requirements usually require at least some time away from home.

Time management is an essential component to the success of all students, regardless of the mode of the program. In the case of the distance learner, we feel that it may be slightly more important. Class time and study time added together with the responsibilities of work and family can really take a toll if it is not considered in the pre-enrollment plans. For example, the majority of the respondents, more than 78%, studied between 11 to 30 hours per week. Add to the mix a family and a regular work week (at least 40 hours) and you have a full schedule.

As is readily apparent, many of our colleagues spent considerable time each week working on school-related issues. Those individuals spending 21 to 30 hours per week studying and also working 40 hours per week had to be masters at time management in order to survive, especially if they were also married and had children. We recommend that if you have not mastered good time management already, you do so prior to enrollment. Consider it to be another requirement for graduation. Students can self-learn time management theory and techniques. Two excellent resources are *Becoming a Master Student* (Ellis, 1994) and *College Learning and Study Skills* (Longman & Atkinson, 1993). Most respondents had families. All of our respondents felt their families played key roles in helping them achieve their goals. Some of their comments about how influential and important their families were follow.

- "They all understood my commitment and supported my efforts."
- "A supportive, encouraging family has definitely made possible the pursuit of my degree."
- "My children were old enough to understand when I had to study. My husband was very supportive by giving me study time, helping with the housework, and taking the boys out so that I could have a quiet study area."
- "[Graduate school] was hardest on my young children. I left before they got out of bed that morning so they wouldn't have to know I was going to class again tonight. I didn't go home after work—just straight to class."
- "The process of including family members is essential to the success of a grad (or any other) student. A great deal of up-front negotiating needs to take place relative to the expectations of family members. Dad was not as available to the kids and spouse as he was previously. Even with considerable dialogue there is still a strong likelihood that conflict will arise."
- "It is an intensive time—seemed that most 'successful' students had strong family (spousal, etc.) support to focus so much time and energy on grad school."
- "Arranging my life was a joint decision with my family—although they disliked my being gone so much."

* "My family was supportive and I used vacation days to study and do research."
* "My wife was taking the same program simultaneously."

We believe that one of the primary keys to successfully complete graduate school is the inclusion of your family in all aspects of your school. Many respondents included their families in a variety of ways: taking them to class or to the library, discussing school with them, including them as part of their support group, studying with their spouses, and having a member of their family type papers for them. Of all of these various inclusionary activities, the one that was most important was having the family as part of a support group. More than 60% of the respondents reported they included their families as part of their support group. More than 85% discussed their graduate school activities with their families. Being a part of a support or discussion group enables family members to feel included and integral to their family member's overall educational plan, thus allowing them some ownership in the process.

It was fascinating to read comments by some of our respondents regarding the participatory nature of their family units. Many of the students felt that their children were being positively influenced as a direct result of a parent or parents enrollment in school. As one doctoral student, a single mother of seven children, stated, "My children would often help me study. They were my cheering team and have gained a great appreciation for the educational process." The opportunity for a child to observe a parent demonstrating strong study skills and a commitment to excel in education is difficult to measure. Several of our respondents reported that their families instituted group study time, akin to the old study hall that Steve can remember as part of his lower-classmen fraternity member requirements. In addition, mothers and fathers were able to discuss with their children career opportunities as they related to education. What an opportunity to seize the teaching moment.

The more you can include your family, the fewer headaches and problems you will have. We are not saying you will live an idyllic life. Graduate school via long distance takes a toll on your family and on you. But the more everyone knows the drill, the better off you will be. Perhaps you can do as one student did: "My husband proofread my papers—mostly fixed all the double spaces after periods. It takes a determination and persistence. My children had to be responsible for

more of the household chores. They had to prepare meals while I was
at class."

NEGOTIATING WITH WORK

Another important aspect of negotiating time is with your employer.
When you first decide to go to graduate school, sit down with your
supervisor or whomever directs staff development traffic at your place
of employment and explain what you are about to do. Get the
commitment up front, not only your employer's commitment to you
but your commitment to your workplace while you are in graduate
school. If you do this as well as discuss your plans with your coworkers, you will quickly discover that the members of your work group
will become your most vocal cheerleaders. Most people want others
to succeed. What we discovered is others wanted to participate in their
own educational programs. Many of our faculty and staff began
undergraduate and graduate programs. Maybe it was because they
thought, "If those two can do it, so can we."

We discovered in our survey that 93% of the respondents worked,
74% of them full-time. For those contemplating graduate school,
understanding that you can complete a degree while working is
significant. Today's graduate schools are looking for students like
those who responded to our survey. Another significant component of
our survey was 84% of the respondents completed graduate programs
part-time. Only 16% completed their programs while enrolled full-time. This means you are not alone. Many people who want to enroll
in graduate programs may feel that working and going to school may
be too overwhelming. It may be, but the key ingredient is that most
of us are in the same educational canoe, sometimes rowing, sometimes
studying, sometimes going to school, sometimes being with our families, and sometimes doing things that need to be done around the
house. The important factor is this: You have people who are going
through the same experiences as you are. Thus, you can support each
other.

It is interesting to note that all respondents to our survey maintained continuous enrollment in their graduate program until completion or are still pursuing their degrees. This seems a little curious to
us. Perhaps those who chose not to respond to the survey did not
because they had "stopped out" or "dropped out."

When negotiating with your employers regarding your graduate program, it might be worth your time to talk about administrative leave. Many companies and colleges allow administrative leave when an employee seeks further education or is involved in staff development. Only 21% of all respondents were actually granted administrative leave, although 65% of all doctoral students received administrative leave. One doctoral candidate explained how she and her employer worked out the details: "My job was very flexible and I could take time as I needed to do classwork or attend classes. Many courses were in line with my job–staff development for teachers." Another graduate student appreciated her school district: "My school board and administration let me leave school 30 minutes early once a week for 2 years." Informing and working with your employer may be the best "course" you ever took.

We chatted with the director of our college about our decision to complete the doctoral program through the University of Idaho. She was elated that we would even consider doing so. She was exceptional. She did expect us to write her a proposal of what we wanted to do, how much time we were going to spend off campus, and how we were going to complete our tasks on our campus. When we needed to spend our time in Boise for our residency, she gave us a week of administrative leave and we took a week of vacation time. When we had to leave early for classes at ISU in Pocatello, she allowed us to leave early. Overall, our institution treated us well. Everyone on campus was supportive and continually asked us how we were doing. When we told them our dissertation topics, many sent us copies of research and other articles about our topics. We probably would not have finished if we had not received the support of our director and colleagues.

Graduate school creates challenges not only for your family but also for your active social life. One graduate student put it succinctly: "My social life diminished drastically. My fitness level also diminished; I'm a very active person and I had to cut way back on physical activities to do my graduate work." When you decide to complete graduate school long distance, you may want to evaluate your life as you now see it. What are you going to do about all the things you have been doing? We would not suggest you cut out everything completely. We discovered you can still exercise and have social interactions with others, albeit in a diminished capacity. Another graduate student wrote, "It was tough to juggle both work and school. There was not much time to do much else." But it is imperative to try to keep some balance in your life. Remember, your job is to complete graduate school in a timely manner, not overwork yourself. You still have other obligations that need to be fulfilled.

As we have discussed, we strongly suggest including your family at every stage throughout the process. Both of us have young families. We still needed to coach T-ball, soccer, basketball, and baseball, and go to plays, recitals, and church activities. Excluding your family can be devastating in the long run. Eat the appropriate food and take time to exercise. When we were completing residency in Boise, we contacted one of the local churches and asked if we could use their gymnasium to play basketball. The clergy was gracious enough to allow us to use the gym to let off 2 hours of steam. By the time we were finished playing one evening, we had forgotten about the rigors of residency and nine credits and had a great time. Other than a sprained ankle, a black eye, a few bruises, and very sore muscles, we had refreshed ourselves. We were ready for the next day. Graduate school, whether it be completed long distance or on campus, is one of the most grueling events you will ever experience in your life, and it is important to take care of yourself along the way.

POINTS TO REMEMBER

* Become a master at time management.
* Include your family in all aspects of your graduate program. Help them understand the importance of graduate school.
* Advise your employer of your goal and negotiate how you will complete your job tasks and your graduate program.
* Advise your family or significant others of your goal. Make sure that everyone understands the time commitment involved in attending graduate school and articulate responsibilities.
* Be realistic when you set up your schedule. Starting off too rapidly can cause you to fail at school, work, or at home.

6

SELECTING YOUR GRADUATE COMMITTEE LONG DISTANCE

*I did not know any of the members except ones I had taken
classes from. I went on their recommendations.*

—PhD student, University of Idaho

Probably one of the most important decisions you will make at the beginning of your gradate program—perhaps the most important decision you will make in graduate school—is the selection of your graduate committee. This chapter focuses on (1) selection of the graduate committee and (2) development and maintenance of relationships with faculty via long distance. As you select your graduate committee, consider the following questions:

* How do I select committee members via long distance?
* What are the interview questions I should ask?
* How many students have they graduated in the past few years?

* How long did it take their students to go through the program and graduate?
* Who should be the chair of my committee?
* What is the best method of communication with him or her?
* How will I need to visit my committee?
* How will I gather them together, especially if they are in different cities and not on campus for consultation purposes?
* Should I ask for a copy of each faculty member's vitae or recent publications?
* Where do I obtain a list of names and telephone numbers of recent graduates. Is it alright to call them up and ask for committee member recommendations?

Selecting graduate committee members is different for doctoral programs and master's programs. As we surveyed and visited with colleagues, we learned that some master's programs did not require a committee. Instead, they may have had an advisor or a committee of two. However, in a doctoral program, most committees are made up of four or more people: your advisor, two individuals from your program emphasis, and at least one person outside your program emphasis. Careful selection of all committee members is critical. You want to finish in a timely fashion. Often, professors have a variety of other activities and may be on other committees. Sometimes, but not very often, things happen between professors that cause them to have a difference of opinion. One doctoral student cautioned, "For long distance schools, it's very difficult [selecting your graduate committee]. It would help to have a 'big sister or brother' who is a local give recommendations. I had to change my committee *twice* so far because the professors don't get along with each other."

The key position is the advisor or committee chair. Chairs are your gurus, your guides, the puppeteers of the rest of the committee. Chairs can hurt you or become the best friend you have ever had. You want the chair as your friend because, ultimately, you want to graduate. In many instances, the best source for selecting your committee members is to go along with the chair's advice. Both of us visited with our chair and asked him for advice. He gave us a list of names that he felt would help us the most in the areas that we were going to be researching.

Probably the best wisdom we can pass along comes from a graduate student. She wrote, "I selected professors who best fit my own personal philosophy." Be a ferret and look around. One doctoral graduate student did a bit of research before she selected her advisor:

"By talking with a classmate who proceeded me in this program. I contacted the person I wanted as my chair; he gave me further input to help with the makeup of the committee." Judiciously select your committee chair. We had the opportunity during one of our summer residencies in Boise to select our committee members. Our major advisor was one of the professors who traveled to Idaho Falls to deliver courses, so he naturally became our advisor because of his proximity, and we saw him almost every week. Thus, he took an active interest in us and our goals to successfully complete the program. The selection of the other three committee members became the challenge.

Before we selected our committee members, we sat down with our major advisor and discussed the potential candidates. We knew that we didn't want to select members located all over the state, so we strategically sought those who were in close proximity. We did not want to have difficulty convening them for meetings. After we listed the names, we then scheduled interviews with faculty members while we were in Boise for our residency. After interviewing them and having them interview us, we then decided who should be on our committees. Many of our cohort group selected all their committee members from the University of Idaho, Boise Center. However, we each selected one committee person from the University of Idaho, Moscow. Steve had done his master's program at University of Idaho, Moscow, and had worked with a variety of individuals. He selected one of his favorite professors there. Darrel had taken some educational administration courses from a particular professor from Moscow who traveled to Idaho Falls to deliver a couple of courses. Darrel enjoyed his philosophy, so he selected him.

You will have to be the one to determine the members of your graduate committee. During the selection process, it is a good idea to review the vitae of potential members. When selecting your committee members keep in mind your needs, and while you are considering the questions to ask potential committee members, consider the following characteristics.

STATISTICS

For some programs, selecting the appropriate statistical tool for scholarly research will be a big headache. Invariably, you will need someone who knows statistics and can help you sort through the various statistical analyses you will be using. As one of our statistics professors said, "If you make a bonehead error, everyone looks foolish in the end. If you make a mistake [in scholarly research], you show your ignorance forever."

CONTENT AREA

You must recognize that even though your committee members are graduate faculty, they may not have expertise in the area you select. Whatever your area of research, you will need someone who has a substantial background in that particular area.

TASK MASTER

You may want a task master, someone to keep you—and your schedule—in line, depending on what type of person you are. If you have a committee member who keeps you focused, you will be better off. Of course, the best task master is yourself. One master's student offered wise counsel: "Choose someone who will challenge you, not just someone you have a good relationship with as a teacher."

GOOD EDITOR

A good editor is a must! Many graduate students can write fairly well. However, when it comes to crossing all the t's and dotting all the i's and making sure this is bold and this is not, editors are nice. Although we were each other's editors, we still had others look over our dissertations. Darrel had a wonderful editor on his committee. Because he is the more subjective writer, he needed someone who could say to him, "Now, Darrel, this is subjective. Don't put it in." It worked for the most part. It might be a wise investment to buy—and use—good software for spelling and grammar checking, but do not rely solely on them. They do not catch everything.

One doctoral student gave some excellent advice: "More time should be spent in selecting committee members so that students can have a committee that is diverse in background and supportive of each other. Everything worked out real well for me but it seems as if the distance relationship with committee members was not as strong as it would have been if I were to have been enrolled in a campus-based program."

In discussing the selection of members of a graduate committee, a master's student said it was "important to know their bias and expectations. Some are more pure research; others want more personal slant to the paper. Know what you want and go for a supportive/challenging committee."

After you select your committee, you then have to have them approved by the graduate school at the university or college. This can either be difficult or easy. When you select committee people, make sure they have graduate status at the university. If they currently do not have approval to serve on graduate committees or teach graduate courses, it may become a difficult and long process to have them obtain graduate-faculty status.

Once the graduate school has approved your committee, you are on your way. Write each member a letter to thank them for accepting a position on your committee. Also, be sure to send each of them your potential topic. They then can watch for research on those topic areas.

COMMUNICATING WITH
YOUR GRADUATE COMMITTEE

During the process of completing a graduate degree, students must discuss a variety of issues with the members of their graduate committee. These discussions may take place face-to-face, on the telephone, or through other mediums. For the most part, respondents to our survey met with their committees one or two times, although many of the master's-level graduate students met with their committees between three to five times. Meeting face-to-face with a graduate committee, especially via distance learning, is a difficult task. Darrel met with his entire committee face-to-face only once. Most of the visits included one or more of the committee members in a telephone conference. When asked about their methods of meeting with their graduate committees, the majority of the survey respondents reported other methods, including telephone interviews, teleconferences, and the use of fax machines. We suspect that with the proliferation of chatting software many graduate students in distance programs will conduct committee interviews via this method.

Many of the respondents to our survey indicated that they informally spoke with their committee chair quite often. Typically, group meetings were arranged only when there was a need to review materials for final approval or when there was a need to deviate from an already approved study plan. One of the MBA students noted on his questionnaire that he met with his committee "quite often—as often as necessary."

The survey showed that the nature and method of communicating to committee members varied widely. The following are some of the responses that we received when we asked the students to describe how they maintained their relationships with the members of their graduate committees.

* "Most of the interaction with committee members was brief and by telephone. The contacts consisted of clarification of the process and recommendations as to how to approach certain questions. The committee members were often times not available and it took a great deal of persistence to make contact with them."
* "By taking classes from each—some in person and some in independent study. I went to campus once in a while to see them and contacted them by phone and e-mail."
* "I initiated the contact by telephone in almost every instance."

Selecting your graduate committee is a key ingredient in finishing your thesis or dissertation. From these comments, you can understand that some had difficult times because of their committee members, and others thought their committee members were the most important elements of the graduate school process. We feel that selecting your committee chair is the most important choice. Whomever you choose, be sure to express thanks and appreciation throughout the process. Good committees spend a great deal of time and energy to help you in completing your thesis, project, or dissertation.

POINTS TO REMEMBER

* The selection of your graduate committee is probably the most important decision that you will make.

* Make certain that the philosophical background of each member of your committee is not in conflict with the project that you wish to conduct.

* Make certain that the members of your committee do not harbor any ill feelings toward one another.

* Establish clear lines of communication with each of the members of the committee. Find out the most effective method of making contact (i.e., telephone, e-mail, snail mail, etc.).

* Select a committee that is made up of individuals who can serve as resource people for each chapter of the dissertation or thesis.

* Understand that the members of your committee most likely sit on several other graduate student and university committees. They are usually full-time faculty members or administrators. They do research and publish. By no means are you the single most important thing in their universe. Because of this, you must take the lead in making certain that all aspects of your program are covered. You cannot rely on them to do everything.

* We recommend that you choose committee members who will allow you autonomy but who will step in and provide critical input when necessary. In other words, do not choose a committee made up of friendly professors who will let you do whatever you choose to do.

7

Developing Support Groups or Cohort Groups

*It is very helpful to have someone who is sharing
the same experiences as you are.*

—MA graduate student, Idaho State University

An important part of any program, graduate or undergraduate, is the developing of support or cohort groups. (We prefer to call them "cohort groups.") It is probably even more important to establish these groups when completing graduate programs long distance. Part of the reasoning hinges on having a person or a group of people become a constant reminder that graduate school is important. In addition, many times you are completing your work in isolation. You may live out in the boonies and no one is around to spur you on. With a cohort group, you will be able to communicate and discuss the rigors of life, liberty, and the pursuit of education.

In addition, when professors are not available, members of cohort groups can offer counsel, discuss specific assignments, help construct courses, and participate in literature reviews. Preferably, the cohort groups should be the same group that is enrolled in the same graduate program. However, students from any graduate program who are doing their programs long distance can offer moral and educational support. Questions about developing support or cohort groups include,

* What kind of cohort group should I be involved in?
* Is this group willing to share travel expenses to and from particular classes or summer residency?
* How tight should I become with this group?
* Should we draw lines or set rules immediately regarding what we are willing to share?
* How and when do these lines change?
* Am I really compatible with this group?
* What is my relationship now with members of this group and how will it change?
* How can my family become a support group?

Our survey included questions that solicited responses regarding cohort groups, and these responses provided some helpful insights. We found that 71% of the graduate students who responded to our survey had formed a cohort group during their program of study. The number of people in the cohort groups ranged from one to more than six. They met in a variety of ways and discussed everything from course-specific topics to personal issues. Most of the respondents reported they discussed work, family, and future the most. It is interesting to note that only 44% said they discussed graduate school per se in their support groups.

Comments and insights regarding the value of the cohort group that were shared by some of the respondents to our survey follow.

* "I believe people seek and provide support as needed to be success-ful; we were all busy with life, work, and school and we helped each other get it done."
* "There were several of us who took classes together and formed acquaintances which might be considered informal cohort groups.

However, we did not meet on an organized basis—only through classes we took together."

* "We met mostly during the dissertation phase. We compared notes on progress, thereby encouraging, supporting, and challenging each other."

* "The cohort group was extremely valuable in providing support and encouragement to complete the program. In addition, group members added significantly to the material learned in the program through personal insights, knowledge, and support."

* "My cohort group got me through the program with my sanity intact!"

* "Our cohort group was developed because of car pool needs— I found invitations to join others would be a drain on what energy I had left—I had no interest in one more 'meeting.'"

* "You need to vent. Venting releases considerable tension and demonstrates how others are going through similar circumstances. We allowed and encouraged this to happen in our cohort group."

* "I think that having someone to motivate you is extremely important."

* "Friendships were established that will last."

For the most part, survey respondents believed that cohort groups were integral to their success in graduate school. One doctoral student wrote, "The cohort group was extremely valuable in providing support and encouragement to complete the program. In addition, group members added significantly to the material learned in the program through personal insights, knowledge, and support."

As noted previously, other graduate students used cohort groups during car pool driving time. For many long distance students, car pools are a necessity. Many used the car pool to vent tensions, frustrations, and other difficulties. But like some car pools, you may need to set rules and boundaries about what you will talk about and what you will not.

More often than not, long distance graduate students who responded to our survey used cohort groups to keep them motivated and interested in the program at hand. Because many of the graduate students worked full-time while enrolled in graduate school, it was important to have someone to motivate them and encourage them to keep plugging along.

POINTS TO REMEMBER

- Cohort groups can provide you with the emotional support essential to your success. The members can be your cheerleaders, study partners, and learning facilitators.
- Members of the cohort group can assist each other in decreasing the cost of education by sharing materials and participating in car pooling.
- Members of the group can provide motivational support and a friendly ear to vent feelings of frustration.
- Cohort groups are an opportunity to develop friendships that can last a lifetime.

REVIEWING LITERATURE LONG DISTANCE WITHOUT LOCAL RESOURCES

I was surprised how many resources were available locally—The search for resources was fun.

—MA graduate student,
St. Francis Xavier Antigomish, Nova Scotia

Key to any research project is establishing a sufficient resource with which to gather literature sources. However, problematic with any long distance program is the area of literature review. Most—if not all—local or regional libraries are not equipped with sufficient resources to conduct a quality review of literature. As you read this chapter, contemplate these questions:

* How do I establish rapport with the local public or school library?
* Does the local library have capability to do computer searches?

* If not, have I budgeted for doing research long distance?
* How will I effectively use interlibrary loans so I can connect with other universities or research facilities to coordinate library loans?
* Is there any way to connect with community college or other local universities in order for me to receive faculty privileges or ways of getting services at colleges at which I am not enrolled?
* Who or what else would be good sources?

Finding a good library with all of the resources you need is a difficult task when you live in rural areas such as found in Idaho. Most community libraries are 1,200 square feet of children's books and have a limited supply of educational research. Fortunately for us we had a university 51 miles south and an excellent private junior college library 24 miles north. Between these two and our own technical library and interlibrary loan, we managed fine.

Interlibrary loan is an important resource. We found librarians love to help you research the information. Interlibrary loan allows you to gather information from a distance by asking libraries in other cities or on other college campuses to loan you a book. If you can extract the information from one of the databases, and you cannot locate the resource at your own library, then interlibrary loan is the way to go. You can ask your librarian to locate the resource from another library. The other library will ship the book to your library, and your library will then loan you the book. Libraries will look up a needed article, photocopy it, and mail it to you. Of course, this comes with a price. Although photocopies may be inexpensive if you do them yourself, photocopies gathered by libraries may be fairly costly. Be sure to ask the costs of any interlibrary loans ahead of time.

The libraries we used had common databases for research—*Social Science Citation Index, Dissertation Abstracts International, Educational Resources Information Clearinghouse (ERIC), Index Medicus,* and so forth. Because the library card catalog has become extinct at most libraries, these databases allow you to search through numerous documents at a high rate of speed. The most common databases are described below.

The *Social Science Citation Index* (SSI) allows you access to more than 300 English-language periodicals published in the United States and abroad. Some of the social science subject areas include anthropology, black studies, economics, environmental sciences, geography, international relations, law and criminology, planning and public administration, political science, psychology, public health, sociology, urban studies, and women's studies.

Dissertation Abstracts International (DAI) is an annual collection of dissertations that have been completed at universities and colleges in the United States. This is a good place to search for what has been done in the area you wish to research.

The Educational Resource Center of the U.S. Department of Education has collected books, reports, unpublished documents, and about 750 journals in education and put all of these documents on a database called "ERIC" for easy access.

The respondents to our survey expressed the need to use a variety of tools in completing their research. Modern technology has made the literature review a new and perhaps much more exciting adventure. With a push of a button, students can have access to hundreds if not thousands of articles to assist them in completing a comprehensive review. One of our colleagues suggested, "The amount of information is so vast that it is overwhelming." Overwhelming indeed; now more than ever the modern researcher must remain focused on the question(s) being asked in the study at hand.

Our colleagues used a variety of types of tools to complete their literature reviews. Almost 80% of them used a college or university library as their primary source to research their topics. It is interesting to note that almost 75% of them used their local libraries, although the local libraries did not have the necessary books on the shelf. More than 67% of the respondents used interlibrary loan. Another key component in researching was the use of colleagues as a source. More than 35% of the respondents stated they used their support groups as sources. While doing our research, we discovered many of our colleagues gathered information for us, especially if they knew our topics. Often when you are looking through the material that abounds in the library or on-line, you come across information that may be vital to a member of your support group. It is easy to copy the information or the source and give it to that person. We are not saying you should be researching someone else's topic. However, if you come across something one of your colleagues is researching, make a note of it and pass it on.

Another important tool in researching is the Internet. Although it was not the most important tool in the research of our survey respondents, it has since become—and will continue to be—an increasingly important tool as more libraries go on-line. Some of the basic Internet sources include search engines such as Altavista (http://www.altavista.com) or Yahoo (http://www.yahoo.com). With any of these searches, all you need to do is type in "ERIC," press enter, and presto—you have access to a wealth of information. Darrel typed in "social science index" and came up with hundreds of bits of information on social sciences. If the information is out there, you will be able to find it. Talk to colleagues and see what types of searches they have conducted on the Internet. Many of them have probably bookmarked certain areas of interest to them. Most browsers allow you to electronically mark a particular website. When you do find a site that has important information for you, be sure to bookmark that site so you will not have to search again for the same site.

In addition, many major universities and colleges have homepages that lead you to libraries, abstracts, entire articles, and so forth. The breadth of your search is limited only by you and the different combination of words you enter in the search.

Initially, we found it interesting that some of the respondents to our survey did not list their university library as a resource. Unfortunately, they did not expand on the answer to this question to let us know what resources *were* used, if any. An analysis of the data gathered for other questions showed that some of the respondents had participated in master's level, nonthesis programs. As a result they were not involved in the process of a literature review. This most likely explains why some of the respondents did not use the university library.

Many of the students used the resources available in their local public library. In one instance, a student let us know that the public library in his hometown had computer stations that could gain access to all of the library resources at a university that was located 45 miles away. This was a big help in doing the literature review; however, it was still necessary for him to make "at least fifty trips to the university's library during the last year" of his program.

Slightly fewer than one third of the individuals who responded to our survey used the resources available to them via the Internet. Unfortunately, many of these colleagues did not have access to the Internet at home. We feel that the Internet will continue to be an ever-increasing resource for distance learners. With a host of libraries going on-line it will enhance access for all those who have the required computers and software. In today's marketplace, you are able to sign up with a local Internet provider for a minimum monthly cost for an unlimited amount of time. If you are going to use a computer and on-line services, be sure to shop around for the best price and service. Shopping for Internet services is the same as shopping for a car or other major purchase. Prior to signing up for Internet services, you must take into consideration the capabilities of your computer hardware and software. It takes some time and research.

It is our feeling that even though many of the respondents did not list their local librarian as being in the top three categories when it came to assisting in the completion of degree requirements, more and more students will rely on librarians in the future. Modern-day librarians are schooled in the latest research technologies. They are your campus experts on how to gain access to information on a variety of topics from a wide range of resources. We had great experiences with the librarians at the local university. The assistance they provided ranged from small group instruction to one-to-one instruction. They delivered short-term instruction that taught us how to effectively use the different databases. On several occasions we were able to benefit from one-to-one assistance that would last anywhere from a quick 2-minute explanation to a half-hour detailed tutoring session. We quickly discovered that strategically planned time with a professional librarian can save an enormous amount of time over the long haul.

More than half of the respondents indicated that they used a personal computer during the completion of the literature review. We are at a time when more and more students who participate in education activities will use the computer as a primary tool. For those of you who are returning to school during middle age, we realize that computers were possibly not an important part of your undergraduate or maybe even your master's program. We, too, can remember the days of manual and electric typewriters, erasable typing paper, and white-out. Those days are gone, though, and we suggest that if you find yourself with minimal or no computer skills as you enroll in your graduate program, you should run—not walk—to the nearest facility where you can enroll in some computer classes that will teach you how to use word processing and spreadsheet software. This will be a wise investment. The review of literature is the foundation of your dissertation. It must be a thorough summary of the body of knowledge that is relevant to your topic, and computer technology will help to make your review as comprehensive as possible.

POINTS TO REMEMBER

- Become familiar with the technology tools that are available to you, including Internet access.
- Participate in classes that are offered, either as a part of your program or in addition to it, that teach you how to use the computer search tools available in your library or through the Internet.
- If you live near a university library, get to know one of the librarians. He or she can help more than you can imagine, and it has been our experience that librarians love to show you how to use the latest tools on the market.
- Become an expert in the use of a personal computer.

MEETING REQUIREMENTS, ENJOYING THE GRADUATION, AND CLOSING THE BOOKS

After finishing the doctoral program, it is just nice to take it easy and atrophy for a bit, maybe do a little fishing, knowing full well I will be jumping pell mell into the next project. I guess that's why I consider myself a lifelong learner. Learning is just like fishing. If you get tired of fishing for a certain kind of fish, you can just head for the next hole, creek, river, or lake. You may catch a few snags once in awhile, but for the most part, fishing—like learning—is always good.

—Long Distance PhD Graduate

This chapter focuses on how graduate students can meet graduation requirements while living away from the university. The first part of the chapter focuses specifically on the dissertation and thesis and how to complete them while completing the degree long distance. The second part of the chapter deals with the other graduation requirements that sometimes are overlooked because the dissertation is the overwhelming graduation requirement. Questions you need to reflect on before you begin the thesis or dissertation process include,

- Have I completed the checklist from the information in the graduate handbook?
- Have I registered with the graduate school for graduation?
- When and where do I take the preliminary or qualifying exams?
- Can I schedule them at my place of business or will I have to travel?
- Will the local community college or library be a testing site?
- What about a proctor in my hometown with the rest of my cohort group?
- How am I going to satisfy residency requirements?
- If residency requires travel, have I made appropriate arrangements with work, family, extracurricular activities?
- Have I completed all the details on my dissertation regarding format, tables, reference list, and so forth, before sending it to the graduate school?
- Who is the person at the graduate school who reviews the thesis and dissertation format? How do I contact that person?
- How many copies do I need to submit?
- What other paperwork is required before I can receive my degree?
- Do I attend graduation?
- Now that I am done, what is next on the agenda?
- How will I continue doing research in my subject area?
- What journals will publish the results of my research?
- Will I be able to conduct workshops or participate in conferences using the results of my research?
- What professional organizations are available to me? Which ones should I join and why?
- What additional professional development activities should I participate in?

REQUIREMENTS FOR DOCTORAL DEGREES

Every undergraduate and graduate program has specific requirements for obtaining a degree. Long distance graduate programs are no different. Graduate programs have a required number of credits beyond the bachelor's degree and have a time limit on the completion of other course requirements.

PROGRAM OF STUDY

After you have selected a major professor and graduate committee, you will need to prepare a formal program of study. Graduate students prepare their study plan after consulting with their major professors and within a couple of semesters of matriculating as a graduate student. The study plan outlines all core coursework, cognate areas, research and statistics courses, and dissertation credits. The graduate school has to approve the study plan. Changes in the program of study can be made later if approved by the appropriate graduate department.

We completed our study plans the first summer of residency. Our cohort group went over all of the academic requirements of our graduate school. After listing all of the courses, we met with our major professor and finalized the plan. Both of us had one or two minor changes during the course of our program, primarily because certain courses we had listed on our programs of study were not offered, so we had to complete courses at other universities.

PRELIMINARY EXAMS

The preliminary examination ("prelims") for a doctoral program is made up of a series of questions based on all your graduate course work. You take the prelims only after you have completed the majority of the courses outlined in your study plan. In our program, each member of our graduate committee submitted a question to our major professor who also prepared one question. As a consequence, we had four questions to answer at our prelims. Each member of the committee had the option of informing us of the areas that the question would encompass. Usually, these questions were relevant to the committee members' fields of expertise. Our committee members chose to divulge the areas that we needed to work on in order to successfully complete the questions, although they discussed the questions only in general terms.

"HI, MOM ... YES, SCHOOL IS GOING GREAT!   I ACED MY PSYCHOLOGY

EXAM THIS MORNING AT UTAH STATE, HAD A GREAT GEOLOGY LESSON

AT STANFORD, TOOK MY LITERATURE MID-TERM AT NORTH CAROLINA...

I HAVE TO GO NOW, MOM, I'm RIGHT IN THE MIDDLE OF MY

MUSIC AND ART APPRECIATION CLASS AT IDAHO STATE!"

Some people may say, "Hey, four questions, that sounds like a piece of cake." However, our prelims, probably like most prelims, embodied a 2-day ordeal that sticks in our minds as one of the most grueling days ever. On the first day, we answered one question in the 3-hour morning block and one question in the 3-hour afternoon block. The second day was a repeat of the first day, only we had two different questions to answer. We had our choice of which question we wanted to answer first, second, third, and fourth. Answering four questions was a difficult task—not the least of which was the taxing ordeal of writing, in long hand, in archaic blue books. Neither one of us had done much long-hand writing prior to the prelims. Computers and word processing numb you to what real writing is.

By noon of the first day, both of our writing hands were sore. By the end of the day, our thumbs and fingers that held our pens had become stuck in the writing position. When we arrived back at the motel where we were staying (we had to travel to Boise to take the prelims), Steve rushed down to the ice machine and got a bucket of ice. Then he thrust his writing hand into the bucket to sooth his aches and pains. By morning, our hands were stiff. The second writing day proved more difficult because our hands and minds were tired. Stopping between paragraphs became more frequent just to rub feeling back in our fingers.

Of the respondents of our survey, only 17% used the computer in completing their preliminary exams. More than 53% used blue books, and another almost 30% did not have to take an exam. As a result of our experience, we strongly suggest that if you have to write your prelims or qualifying exams long hand, make sure to practice months before the exam. We would hope you can convince your graduate committee to allow you to use technology to write your exams instead. Tell the members of your committee that you will buy a diskette from them so they do not think you are bringing your responses to the examination room.

Many graduate programs do allow the use of computers to complete their preliminary exams. Either the student or the department provides the computer. In addition, sometimes the preliminary examination is not in the traditional essay format. Instead, examinations may take the form of a portfolio that is a compilation of a variety of papers, essays, or other types of work you have completed during the program. Other graduate programs require a single big paper on some subject that you and your committee decide on. It is important for you to do some research about your options. Visit with your department or graduate committee chair about departmental-approved options for taking your prelims; you may discover an option that best suits your situation. After you successfully complete your prelims, you are "advanced to candidacy."

RESIDENCY

Residency is the number of credits needed to be completed on campus or at an approved off-campus site. The question usually arises about where the student spends residency. In our doctoral program, we spent residency in Boise, 270 miles from Idaho Falls. Our residency was 2 weeks during two summers, with nine credits each summer. Some of our cohort group who completed their doctoral programs in educational administration served their residency in Idaho Falls. However, the inconsistency has been resolved, and Idaho Falls has become a residency center for all other doctoral students. Many distance programs do not require a formal residency period. If this is one of your challenges, then do some exploring into the graduate program that allows you to accommodate your needs.

Not all respondents of the survey spent time in residency to complete their graduate degrees. Only 9% of the master's-level students had to spend time in residency. All doctoral students spent some time in residency, ranging from 5 weeks to more than 20 weeks.

PROPOSAL

After you have completed your preliminary examination and completed residency, you are ready to begin—or in some cases complete—the proposal-writing stage. The proposal encompasses an overview of your dissertation, written in pseudo-dissertation form, with all of the appropriate chapters. After completing your proposal, you submit it to your committee chair for approval. On receiving approval, you then send copies of your proposal to your committee members. They review the chapters, determine whether your research questions are appropriate, viable, and narrow enough in scope to be addressed. Your entire committee meets with you to discuss the pros and cons of your proposal. This is the time to ask questions. In this setting the committee members are more than willing to guide you. They also assist the neophyte researcher in making sure you do not set yourself up for failure. Of course, this process may vary from one graduate program to another.

Some rumors exist that committee members are out to "get you." In ours and our cohorts' experiences, it is just the opposite. All of our committee members were interested in seeing us succeed. Granted, they asked difficult questions and made us work hard, but they helped us step by step and answered any questions we asked.

DISSERTATION

Finalizing the application process, completing the coursework, driving to and from your courses, writing preliminary examinations, and completing your proposal are just precursors to the biggest challenge you probably will ever face in your life: the dissertation, the big "D." If your graduate program requires the dissertation, it will be the biggest hurdle to cross. That is why many doctoral students do not complete the dissertation and finish their educations with the "ABD," (a.k.a. "all but dissertation"). For some reason, writing a dissertation can create the worst excuses known to humankind. Procrastination is probably the biggest culprit of all. It is plain easier to do something else. Also, the topic one picks may be part of the problem. We strongly suggest that you choose a topic that you really like, because you will be spending an extraordinary amount of time researching, discussing, writing about, and reflecting on this topic. If you do not like your topic, you could be in for a rough time in finishing your dissertation. All of us who have finished have gone through this process. We are thankful that our cohort groups were always around to ask us, "So how's your dissertation going?" Sometimes more out of guilty feelings or wanting to be able to talk about the progress of the dissertation, you complete the big "D."

Steve had a unique way of writing his dissertation. He wrote on his survey:

> The time during the process went very fast. My approach was to take things one step at a time and not to think about the total picture. I believe that this allowed me to remain motivated to accomplish small tasks along the way and to keep from being overwhelmed. As an aside . . . sometimes I would put in long hours to complete writing assignments for classes and also during the dissertation phase of the process. Fortunately, my place of work has a long hallway so . . . when

I got feeling a little tense or was experiencing some "writer's block" I would go out into the hall and do some wind sprints, then go back to writing. Of course, this did not take place during the normal working hours of the college. Typically, this would happen early on Saturday mornings or late at night.

Most of us, if not all of us, in writing dissertations and theses spent a great deal of time in front of the computer, late at night or early in the morning or both, trying to finalize everything. Sometimes, the computer did not cooperate. Darrel was writing one night late and his computer got an appetite and started eating his tables. After a rather excited few moments, he reached over and shut off the machine—better lose some of it rather than all of it, was his philosophy. The next morning, after he had calmed down and apologized to the world for becoming so irate, he turned on the machine. Lo and behold, it was back to normal.

A master's student had an even worse nightmare. He pressed "delete this page," and his machine deleted his entire thesis. One punch of the button, and *swoosh!*—gone. So one bit of advice: *Always* save your documents to a floppy disk, maybe even two hard copies. You should also save to the hard drive, maybe in a couple of places. Saving documents will take you longer, but lose about a page or more and you will pat yourself on the back for taking the extra time. Knowing you have extra copies of everything will allow you to sleep at night. However, remember to save the same draft on the various diskettes and the hard drive. Both of us saved to the hard disk every 3 minutes or so, and then saved to a floppy disk every so often. You do not want to be running down the long hallways at work, pounding your fist on the walls. Someone might hear you and call the police.

The majority of the graduate students who responded to the survey completed the lion's share of their dissertation or thesis at home. Slightly fewer than 10% of the respondents reported that they were able to complete most of their writing at work. Some of the comments in this section related to the fact that those who were able to complete most of their dissertation or thesis at work did so because of the close relationship between their topic and the focus of their work. For instance, one of our colleagues studied the types of employee learning styles preferred by employers. The individual addressing this question was employed as a career planning and placement officer at a college, which fit nicely with his dissertation topic.

Employer interviews and workshops that were conducted for his dissertation also satisfied some of the requirements of his job. Being able to complete a dissertation, or even coursework for that matter, constitutes the optimum scenario for a person to be actively using knowledge gained in the pursuit of a degree and simultaneously meeting the demands of his or her employer.

Finishing a dissertation is probably one of the best feelings ever. For us it was like a spiritual epiphany. Darrel remembers when he finished and placed everything in an overnight express box and mailed it to his major professor. He walked outside of the express mail office in a blinding blizzard and thought the heavens had opened up on him. Finishing resembles the feeling of enlightenment. You are done!

However, the feeling of not finishing can be the most miserable feeling you have ever felt. One of our cohorts has not yet completed her dissertation. Her feelings reflect the worst of the experience.

> It would be interesting for me to find others who have not completed their dissertation. I feel like a failure for starting something that I haven't finished. But having come this far I also don't feel intelligent enough to even start a dissertation. It would be another failure on my part. Moms don't need PhDs but patience. Unless there is support from inside the home it seems an insurmountable task! Since there may be others like me who will read your book I'd suggest some sort of family questionnaire or contract to evaluate support before education is attempted. Do an orientation/picnic/etc for *families* at the beginning or make an orientation pamphlet for families discussing support, ways to help the student, how to be more independent at home, etc.

Writing a dissertation was a wonderful, enlightening experience for both of us. Writing can be therapeutic as well as nostalgic. The bottom line is this: "Get ready to rewrite, rewrite, rewrite" and get ready to stay up late and feel some of the most excruciating pain and joy you have ever felt in your entire life. One of the doctoral students put it this way: "A person must go through the process in order to understand the difficulty of the task!"

An excellent book on surviving the dissertation process is Rudestam and Newton's (1992) *Surviving Your Dissertation: A Comprehensive Guide to Content and Process.* Rudestam and Newton outline the process, from getting started, to working with content, to what you need to know to make your dissertation easier to write.

"FRIENDS FINALLY FOUND ROGER HOURS
LATER, WITH HIS FINGER STILL FROZEN
ON THE 'PAGE DELETE' KEY."

YOUR DEFENSE

Even after your dissertation is done, you are not quite finished—yet. Although the rest may seem like a formality, you still have to prepare for the defense of your dissertation or thesis. On completion of your dissertation, and after your committee has reviewed the final version, you set up your defense. At the defense, the graduate committee can ask you any question about anything about your dissertation or project. Your defense date is published in the college's bulletin, so if people want to attend and listen to your defense, they can.

Setting up the defense of your dissertation can be especially tricky for those of us who completed our entire graduate programs long distance. Darrel's was challenging to say the least. He called all of the graduate committee members to coordinate the time schedule. He was in Idaho Falls, three members were in Boise, and the fourth member lived in Lewiston, Idaho, some 50 miles or so from Moscow. At the defense, everyone was there, except for the committee member from Lewiston. The major professor had arranged for a teleconference with the member from Lewiston.

Steve created a table that listed 2-weeks worth of possible dates for the defense. The table was mailed to each of the committee members with instructions to mark the dates that they were not able to conduct a defense, then mail it back. The committee members followed through and with very little effort a date was established that was convenient for all.

Another way you may be able to schedule the defense is to put together a calendar of dates and times. Circulate a copy or an e-mail version of the calendar to all members of your committee. Have them block off times they will *not* be available during that week(s) and return the pages to you. When you receive the responses back, then you can schedule suitable times for the meeting. Having some sort of plan will eliminate enormous amounts of time in calling or talking to voice mail.

On the day of our defenses, we drove to Boise early in the morning, defended at 1:00 p.m., and then drove home afterward, a total of 540+ miles round trip. Because most of the committee members had other obligations, our defenses were set for a specific block of time. We figured if we talked enough, there would not be enough time for anyone to ask questions. On the contrary! Our committee members asked us various questions. Sometime during the defense, the committee asked for a couple of things to be changed in our dissertations. After the questions were asked and then answered, they invited us to leave the room while they discussed whether we could become "Doctors."

The other sweet feeling, besides finishing the dissertation, is when that door opens to the conference room and your major professor steps out into the foyer and says, "Dr. Hammon (or Dr. Albiston), congratulations! Why don't you come join us." We walked back into the room where we were heartily congratulated. The first thing we both did when the defense was over was to call our wives. Darrel called his and said, "Well, Mrs. Hammon, you are now the wife of a Doctor." When Steve called his wife, she let out a wild squeal and congratulated him. Just to hear our wives' congratulatory remarks make it all worthwhile. The 258-mile drive from Boise back to Idaho Falls was the fastest trip in the world. Both of us experienced a sense of euphoria.

The day we returned to work, we encountered thunderous applause, gifts, banners, shouts of elation and congratulations, and e-mail messages. Our college faculty and staff bent over backward to make us feel like we had accomplished one of the most difficult tasks ever. And we felt we had, too. Everyone at the college called us "Doctor" for several days afterward. It felt awkward and still does. We like to be called "Darrel" and "Steve."

After the exhilaration of completing the degree and all of the celebrations associated with the event, one can expect to feel a little strange, perhaps more aptly described as a feeling of loss. We had a hard time relaxing in the months immediately following completion of our program. When we would try, it seemed as if we should have been busy doing something, like working on our dissertation or reading more research or crunching more numbers and building tables. You shouldn't worry about this phenomenon, but just be aware of it, so that when it happens you will not be taken by surprise. We fondly refer to it as the post-dissertation blues.

STILL NOT DONE

When you think you are done with the dissertation or your graduate work, you really are not. Even after graduation ceremonies, you still need to make sure your dissertation or thesis is in the hands of the graduate school. There is a variety of forms you will need to sign and send to them. Your dissertation has to be approved by your committee chair and dean of the graduate school. Plus you need to send your dissertation or thesis to the library with a signed consent so they can put it on microfilm. One of the main documents you need to sign and send in before or after your defense, usually before, is your "authorization to graduate" form. This allows you to go to the graduation exercises. If you decide to attend your graduation exercises, which we strongly suggest you do, then you will need to order your cap and gown through the mail and pay the money. We also suspect that there will be other paper requirements at the institution you choose. Make sure you review those and compose a checklist. You can't afford not to complete one of the forms. Most graduate schools are sticklers about getting all the paperwork complete and in. And we were supposed to become a paperless society!

When all of the paperwork is done, your dissertation submitted, graduation over, your university or college will send you a copy of your diploma. Make this an event. Darrel's wife called him and told him his diploma had arrived. Steve had gone home for lunch and there it was sitting in his mailbox. Being able to finger our diplomas was an amazing experience. We thought about the number of hours we had spent in class, driving to and from classes and residency, and the time we spent before the computer god. We did all of that for a piece of 11" x 14" parchment. Yes, it was worth it!

MOST USEFUL COMPONENT IN COMPLETING GRADUATION REQUIREMENTS

When asked to prioritize the most useful component in completing graduation requirements, respondents to our survey rated committee chairs, family, and self as the most useful. Respondents reported that of these they found their committee chair to be the most helpful in assisting them in completing graduation requirements. It is easy to understand why this would be the case, because the committee chair is responsible for reviewing the initial study plans and thesis or dissertation topics prior to gaining the approval of the entire committee. The committee chair is the one who directs traffic and makes contact with the other committee members.

However, we found it to be somewhat interesting that the committee members in general received such a low rating in the survey. In our cases, the chair did do a lot of work facilitating the process, taught many of the courses we took, and directed our summer residency in Boise. However, the other members of the committee were consulted along the way and provided an enormous amount of input. The respondents reported that they felt that after the chair, their families and themselves were the most instrumental in their success. This causes one to wonder about the metal of graduate students in general and those who complete a distance learning program. Could it be that distance learners have a greater sense of self-reliance? We posit that they do and feel that this would be a fascinating as well as insightful research question to address in the future.

ENJOYING THE GRADUATION—CLOSING THE BOOKS

As one graduate MAT student said, "I may have a piece of paper designating a degree, but I hope to never close the books on my university career—wherever the campus."

The purpose of this section is to finalize attending graduate school long distance and some of the loose ends that need to be completed. Part of any program is bringing to closure the termination of the degree. However, with the techniques students have learned through obtaining a degree through long distance programs, they will be able to continue the lifelong pursuit of educational happiness. Professional development must never end. As technology and knowledge continue to increase, students should never close the books on their education. Rather, being a part of and graduating from a graduate program should propel them into doing additional research in their fields of interest.

ATTENDING GRADUATION EXERCISES

When we conducted our survey, we were interested in learning how many of the graduate students who completed their degrees via long distance learning actually attended their graduation ceremonies. In discussing graduation ceremonies in general with our cohort group during our program of study, we learned that many of our peers did not attend graduation for their undergraduate degrees and in some cases they did not attend for the master's degree. This held true even though most of them completed their degrees in residence. Our cohort group, almost unanimously, expressed the desire to attend the graduation ceremony should they complete their doctoral or master's program. However, the data from our survey showed that slightly fewer than 50% of the graduates attended their graduation ceremonies. We feel that this is a fairly substantial figure in light of the number of miles some individuals had to travel in order to attend. In our case, we traveled more than 500 miles!

It was an awesome experience to stand at the edge of the stage, dressed in full doctoral regalia, as the title of our dissertation was read. Then we sauntered to the center of the stage where we met our major professor. We bowed just a bit while he stood behind us and placed the doctoral hood over our heads and adjusted it on our shoulders. We embraced and said pleasantries. We walked to the dean of the graduate school and shook hands while camera lights flashed. Then we made the short walk down the ramp and off the stage and into the arms of our best support persons: our wives. Truly, this was the culmination of a long, arduous journey.

One could infer that the task of completing a degree long distance creates a greater need for a ceremony for reward and celebration and to bring closure to a lengthy process. One master's student expressed her reasoning for attending her graduation ceremony: "Graduation was not only for me but for my family. I was hoping to set an example for my young sons. Even though we sat for three hours, I'm glad I did graduation!" Although most of the graduates felt attending graduation was an important part of "closing the books," one respondent stated, "It was just a hurdle I needed—the ceremony is a meaningless process to me!" But the comments of two graduate students echoed the majority of the respondents' comments: "Chose to attend graduation to 'finish off' my investment" and "*Gracias a Dios*" ("thanks to God").

PUBLISHING AND PRESENTING

Another topic of interest to us in conducting our survey was to find out if our colleagues had taken the information learned during the course of graduate school and published parts of their dissertation or thesis. Initially, it was somewhat of a surprise that many of them had not. After we read the narratives in the survey, it became clear that, for the most part, the respondents to our survey had not been out of school for too long and perhaps may not have had the time to publish. As one of the respondents put it, "Come on you guys! Give me a break, I just barely graduated!"

Even though many of our colleagues have not published parts of their dissertation or thesis, several indicated an interest in doing so, and a couple of them stated they were in the process of completing drafts of their research in publishable form.

Akin to publishing research is sharing it in the form of workshops or presentations. Approximately 25% of the respondents to our survey had presented materials related to their dissertation or thesis. One of our colleagues has been able to present at four different professional seminars, three in the United States and one in a foreign country, within 8 months of completing a doctoral program. We would suggest that this person is the exception rather than the norm.

So much valuable information is gathered and synthesized in the process of completing a dissertation or thesis. Many of your colleagues will be eager to hear what you have found. Please share your information in publications or workshops. Our advice is that you think about this prospect as you are going through your program. Also, attend workshop and conference sessions that deal with your topic in some way. Talk to the presenters. Usually, they have had to complete research on their presentation topics but probably might be willing to share or even help you prepare your research for dissemination. Perhaps being in tune to the prospect of publishing will give you some good ideas along the way.

CONTINUING EDUCATION

Besides publishing and presenting, in what other activities do individuals schooled via distance education participate? One question that we asked in our survey was whether our colleagues had enrolled in any other classes since completing their degree, and if so what type of class. We found that many of the people who had completed their degree had enrolled in some kind of a class since graduating. Most respondents stated they would continue to take courses, both academic and "fun" courses such as painting. When asked the types of classes actually taken since completing a graduate degree, almost 25% of the respondents said they had taken or were currently taking a recreational course; 18% more reported taking graduate courses (these are the die hards!), and almost 9% reported taking self-help courses.

OTHER ACTIVITIES

Completing graduate school, whether it be long distance or on campus, takes a toll. When some of the respondents finished their programs of study, they did things they had not done for a long time. For example, Darrel went on a long vacation, something he had not done in 5 or 6 years. Because his fourth-grade daughter was going to be studying Idaho history, they went on an Idaho tour, traveling around the state. Steve put money down on a new Harley Sportster, his graduation present to himself.

The continued interest in taking classes supports the lifelong (perpetual) learning philosophy adhered to by our fellow students. In addition, almost one third of the students had enrolled in recreational or self-help classes. It is hard to determine the real reason the students continued to enroll in classes. This is yet another topic for further research. Do graduates enroll because of a yearning for continued learning or is it the result of the need for continued social interaction? Or are they addicted to education? Perhaps the reason varies depending on the type of class that the graduate takes. We will leave these questions and more for another time.

POINTS TO REMEMBER

- Every graduate program has specific requirements for graduating. Make sure that you understand every aspect (i.e., transfer credit requirements, number of required credits for each component, and residency requirements).
- Get approval of your study plan as soon as possible.
- Find out how the preliminary examination will be conducted and prepare yourself accordingly. Visit with your committee members about potential questions or areas of study.
- Keep on task while working on your dissertation. Set many benchmarks to be completed with specific time deadlines and then follow them religiously. Do not procrastinate.
- Keep your committee, especially your committee chair, apprised of your status. Make certain that you plan a date for your defense well in advance. Each institution has a cut-off date each semester.
- Do not forget that there is a lot of paperwork that needs to be submitted to the graduate school during your last semester of enrollment in order for you to graduate. We advise that you make a checklist of everything that is required of you and then check off each item as you complete it.
- Be prepared for the post-dissertation blues.
- Identify and enlist the support of the people who can assist you in reaching your goal.
- Celebrate the completion of your dissertation.

- Attend your graduation ceremony if at all possible and include the members of your family. This is definitely the culmination of your graduate program.
- Publish the results or portions of your study and conduct related workshops so that the information that you have gathered may be shared.
- You may find yourself continuing to take classes just for fun or to continue to stretch your mind!

10

A PERSPECTIVE FROM PROFESSORS OF DISTANCE LEARNING

Going beyond the walls is a most important and consequential procedure. It helps to demolish the foolish tradition that there is no intelligent life beyond the campus. It carries with it many implications of developing new playing fields which also result in access-equity challenges. The physical way in which the many groups of students in far-off classrooms are shown and can interact on the screen helps create in everyone's mind the sense of community of learners in many places joined together in the same quest. Unlike the single classroom, where students see the professor's face and the backs of other students' heads, we are all face to face on the screen! That helps to promote interaction.

—G. Bensusan, e-mail, July 24, 1996

As we were writing the various chapters of this book, we discovered we left out one important chunk of information—the insight that can be obtained by the professors who provide distance education courses.

Many snippets have been written about the attitudes of traditional higher education, about its lethargy and historical adherence to the traditional, the lecture, the students in class, the giant lecture halls. But what really is occurring, in our experience at least, is that purveyors of higher education, for the most part, are looking out over the lecture halls and thinking, "Tradition is still a viable source, but what must we do to serve those who cannot make it to the great lecture halls before us?" This attitude is a changing paradigm—a much-needed change. Movement in the trenches can be slow, but any movement forward is positive. The professors who teach long distance courses have the vision of the future, because they are developing it.

We sent professors a short list of questions and asked them to share their thoughts on distance learning. One of the questions we posed to the professors was, "How do you feel about extending the campus to outreach sites?" From a professor from the University of Wales, Bangor, came the response: "It is a moral duty and a political imperative to sustain lifelong learning and extend opportunity to all, and not just those who can attend or live near a campus university" (M. Owen, e-mail, July 23, 1996). Although many felt the obligation to extend courses to outreach, there was a message to further extend "collaboration and expertise" to smaller institutions.

Preparing to teach a course long distance received candid feedback. "Yes" was the resounding response to the question of whether it took more time preparing for long distance courses. However, many felt that time spent on developing course materials for a larger audience seemed to breed efficiency, especially if professors produced a bound copy of the materials.

Darrel and Richard Sparks from Idaho State University taught via long distance for almost 3½ years on "ABE on TV" (Adult Basic Education television) and experienced a different type of preparation. They taught a variety of subjects from adult learning theory, adult basic education, Internet for literacy providers via a television program sponsored by the local Public Broadcast System (PBS) station, and other related topics. The program ran each semester at 8:00 a.m. on Saturday mornings at the Pocatello station, and Darrel drove down each morning at 6:30 a.m. and returned at 10:00 a.m. Every Friday at 4:00 p.m., for an hour or more, they "practiced" the show. Because the focus of the program was tied to technology, they produced all materials on presentation software programs.

During the spring 1996 semester, they broadcast from different sites. Richard was at his site in Pocatello, and Darrel was in Idaho Falls.

On one occasion they brought in another colleague from the North Idaho College campus in Coeur d'Alene, Idaho, about 580 miles north of Idaho Falls. We searched the Internet for literacy sites that outreach literacy councils could gain access to and use. Overall, the program was a huge success, and people, including teachers and administrators from several school districts, participated. Because the program was also classified as a talk show, students could call in on the toll-free telephone. The use of snail and e-mail and the telephone brought together a variety of people who otherwise would have never known about what was "out there."

As Darrel experienced, one of the biggest challenges in teaching this kind of course was traveling. Many professors traveled great distances to teach. The professors who came to Idaho Falls to instruct our cohort group traveled between 270 and 520 miles per trip per class time. Some felt the time was spent unproductively, although those who car pooled with another professor to the same site discussed education and probably had more time to finally talk about the larger issues.

Some of the professors mentioned that historically being on campus built community. But we must remind ourselves the communities are different than they were many years ago when campuses were first founded and constructed by religious leaders to link and strengthen the religions. We have come "from afar" and still seem afar off. One distance learning professor posited that although some schools are part of the local lore of life, going to college creates surrogate communities, ones in which people live, sleep, go to school, eat, do laundry, go on dates, attend any sports event imaginable, become addicted to drugs, get pregnant, and, it is hoped, learn something well enough so they can market themselves to present to potential employers.

One distance learning professor stated,

> The convergence of television and computers . . . depends on literacy of some sort in the user. We are going for apartheid on a larger scale than South Africa could ever have dreamed of, although on a slightly different criteria. . . . The "next revolution" is going to leave the have-nots even farther behind than ever before . . . telecommunicated learning is not going to solve the inequities of the world. But I would argue that it is going to help level the playing field even more than did the evolution of the mass print media. Not next year, but perhaps within a generation—maybe less, given the exponential

development of technology. (M. B. Goldstein, Internet posting, July 12, 1996)

Not all professors who work in long distance programs think it is the most wonderful thing since sliced bread. In fact, one of our own professors had major reservations about doing distance learning long distance:

> I am not an advocate of physically taking courses to off-campus sites. I know that the argument for extending the campus is that people cannot get away from their jobs to attend campus programs, and as a consequence, the number of doctorates would decrease. While that argument is true I am not too certain that the resulting consequences would be undesirable. I believe that the single biggest disappointment in my doctoral program was realizing that after resigning a teaching position and leaving hearth and home to attend a "quality" program virtually all of the coursework was offered in the evening to accommodate the folks who had to make a living and couldn't leave their employment. The only balancing factor was that most of those who couldn't get away from their jobs to go to the campus also, after graduating, couldn't get away from their jobs to reap the benefits of their accomplishment.

One major advisor, stated the matter succinctly when he noted, "Those who leave the hooding ceremony to return to the same job they had when they enrolled in the program did not get an education—they got in-service training."

We asked additional questions of the professors that merit a paragraph or two.

Question: Do You Have to Prepare More to Teach a Course Long Distance?

Preparing to teach a course long distance takes more time. Most professors we know and those faculty members who teach long distance on our campus use a variety of technology. One such tool is Microsoft's presentation software, PowerPoint. Preparing a PowerPoint presentation takes time, especially if you use all of the bells and whistles that come with the 7.0 version. One professor stated,

> Yes, both in quantity and quality. Since I work with many sites simultaneously and what with fire alarms, electronic breakdown or

something else going wrong, I have to be prepared to flip-flop my lessons in whatever direction is necessary. In a single classroom you can get away with dismissing class, but when nine classrooms full of people at different state sites have each driven ten to fifty miles to get there, it is important that they not be turned away. Even if you stand in your classroom alone and make a presentation to a camera, you can fulfill the need for the students, and it also shows you care. That means plans A, B, C, and sometimes D—*flexibility.* Preplanning is also necessary to make sure you get all the necessary class materials to all sites in advance. No second-class citizenship can be allowed!!! (G. Bensusan, e-mail, July 24, 1996)

One of our professors, when asked about preparation for his long distance learning course, asked about what the word "prepare" meant: "If the term is defined in the narrow sense of organizing content knowledge and presentation points for a lesson the answer is no. If the definition includes getting from the office to the classroom the answer changes to a resounding YES!"

▨ Question: Are Your Long Distance Students Different Than Your "Campus" Students in Terms of Output, Dedication, Motivation, and So Forth?

We received a variety of responses to this question. One professor stated that most of his long distance students were employed full-time during their coursework. He also mentioned that two of his best students were mothers. He conjectured that they probably did not have any more or less time than their employed counterparts. Rather, they probably were able to control their time more efficaciously.

Another professor stated that most of his long distance students were "older, professionals, empty nesters." Many of his students demonstrated "superior" quality. He also mentioned that many of his "campus students" were a bit miffed about not being the focus of his attentions. However, as time went on that changed somewhat, although they still became disturbed when he actually transmitted from the off-campus site to the campus site. He also maintained, "Many of the *best* student are at distant sites: professionals, highly motivated, deeply responsible both in doing their assignments and keeping up with the videotapes when they have to miss class. That "superiority" also creates some friction—with all the advantages of on-campus access to library etc., the off-campus students *often* shine. I use that reality as a way to stimulate more effort from the locals."

■ Question: Is Travel Involved in Teaching Your Courses?
Does This Add to the Burden or Does the University
Compensate You for the Travel?

Many long distance professors have to travel to an off-campus site.
It is part of the realm of doing business and taking the courses to the
customers who live in the outreach area. Some professors believe that
being able to travel to outreach sites improves class interaction. When
professors spend 1 week at each site and then rotate from site to site,
they have time to spend with outreach students. During the time they
are off campus, they are able to help students one-on-one and,
according to a professor, "help them develop their awareness of their
local course resources—part of my effort to diminish system-wide
access inequities!"

Our experience with professors off campus was varied. We had
the opportunity to visit one-to-one with all of our professors. On a
couple of occasions, we met one of them in his hotel room and chatted
about course work and other peripheral topics. Often, just chatting
with professors offers another way to get to know them as people, not
just as ivory-tower, pedagogical-(andragogical, in our case) touting
academicians. They are real people with real concerns. They expressed
how tired they became traveling to Idaho Falls each week. Traveling
that much took a toll on their home lives as well. We probably met
more with our professors, one-to-one, in our doctoral programs than
we ever did during our undergraduate and master's programs.

Long distance professors have other concerns about teaching long
distance courses, especially if travel is involved. These concern class-
load and ability to do what needs to be done. One concerned professor
lamented,

We . . . have the same teaching load, in credit hours, as a campus
faculty member, which is nine credit hours. We also have the same
research and service requirements for tenure and promotion as
campus-housed faculty. It doesn't take a deep philosophical thinker
to realize that with the loss, every week, of at least one full working
day to travel, the only way an off-campus member can hope to
compete is to use the weekends to do it, in the areas of research and
service, what campus faculty can do during the week. Obviously, since
both positions are allocated 168 hours per week by the Master
Planner, the off-campus member simply cannot compete with a
campus member who also devotes his or her weekends to professional
development. Before anyone jumps to the simplistic conclusion that

the solution to this dilemma is to cut the course load or reduce the promotion and tenure standards for off-campus faculty, let me hasten to offer the invariable consequences of that action. Cutting the teaching load would result in every credit offered off campus costing the taxpayers *at least* 50% more than equivalent campus offerings. The consequences of reducing the tenure and promotion standards for off-campus faculty members are too obvious to require comment.

Question: Do You Use E-mail and the Internet to Communicate With Your Students? Are There Other Ways to "Chat" With Your Students?

Most, if not all, professors use e-mail and the Internet as tools to communicate with their students. But one of the challenges that arose in the discussions was the "unlevel playing field" of the graduate students.

Not everyone has access to on-line research, the Internet, or even e-mail. One professor stated that "three sites out of ten have *excellent* access, three more have *good* access, and four have access limited to phone and faxes." One professor stated he only used e-mail to communicate with students during the dissertation phase, although he has had very few students with sufficient skills to use the technology. With one student, he used e-mail exclusively to edit her dissertation. The student mailed her dissertation draft as a WORD DOC attachment. Then the professor made his corrections using "annotation" and "revision" functions in his word processing program and then e-mailed it back to the student. During each editing, he was able to use the "document compare" function to determine precisely how she had handled each case. The professor also made one important observation about the type of students who are able to effectively use the technology:

> Let me hasten to add that not every student has the technological *savoir-faire* to handle such a task. . . . Obviously, I could insist on my students being able to deal with innovations in computer technology, but it is not good to have individual faculty members placing serendipitous requirements on students. The result is generally a mass migration to a less demanding advisor. In order for standards to "work," they *must* be imposed by university authority—or at the very least, college administration authority.

▨   Question: What About Dissertations, Graduate Committees,
    and So On—How Do You Deal With Those Long Distance?

This question did not bring as much insight as we had hoped.
Perhaps, this was the sore spot for most. For us, it was the most difficult
part of our program, mainly because of the number of telephone calls,
the driving, and so on. For the most part, professors met with their
students in their hotel rooms, restaurants, and after class. One professor said,

> Hopefully the potential of chatting [defined as being able to converse
> with another person or a group of persons via software that allows
> for conversation] and compressed video will be realized in the not
> too distant future. At the risk of sounding totally pessimistic, how-
> ever, I would have to note that our poor use of television and our lack
> of capability to use technological innovations in our existing class-
> rooms does not seem to offer too much basis for hope.

▨   Question: What Is the Future of Distance
    Learning and Long Distance Education?

According to professors of long distance courses, the future of
long distance learning has nowhere to go but up. One professor even
used the term "decentralized learning" for distance learning. Some of
the differences may be the rural versus metropolitan. Some universities
in the United States are trying to deliver courses to sites that will be
within 30 minutes of a distance learning site. One of the important
movements in distance learning will be the development of these
courses on the World Wide Web (WWW). One professor offered these
reasons why developing WWW courses would be better in metropolitan areas: "(1) better hookups, (2) more variety of providers, (3) better
economy [people can afford and get easier access to computers,
services, and maintenance], (4) greater incentive to stay at home and
avoid traffic, muggings, etc."
    One of the major problems with long distance learning, according
to one of our respondents, is that "the future is coming at us faster
than we can absorb it" (G. Bensusan, e-mail, July 24, 1996). The
potential to transmit long distance learning courses to students is
immeasurable. At our college, we have not even begun to tap all of
the resources. We have many students who live in our communities
who are underprepared or unprepared to work in today's market-

place. Students throughout the country do not even know what they want to learn—yet—but the dreams are there. In addition, business and industry have employees who need to upgrade their skills to meet the demands of integrating new technology. What long distance learning does is open up new avenues and conduits for people who normally do not have direct access to these services. As one professor responded to our questions,

> If the advances being made in communications can be harnessed and used by universities, it seems to me that there is a cause for real hope for developing effective and efficient distance learning techniques. On the other hand, we may find that the inability or lack of desire of university faculty to use innovations results in a movement back to strictly campus-based graduate programs. I can see virtues in either one of these outcomes, and I believe that the relentless pruner of the inefficient which we refer to as "the market" will move us in the right direction, whatever that direction may be. The speed with which the market will move us toward efficiency and effectiveness is inversely proportional to the amount of resources which meddling authorities are willing and able to devote to achieving their own ends, which may or may not be the ends the market demands.

Other comments regarding the future of distance education follow.

* "There will be multiple speeds and breadths of transition. Just as many delivery systems currently exist, they will evolve variously, across a broad front, with each sector distinctive based on its antecedents. Stasis may be a thing of the past—perhaps even traditional professors in their closed-door classrooms will evolve when virtual is in the air. I see this as *very* positive, creating access in many new ways, with potential students freed from the preexisting lockout which accompanied the older system. But then, maybe I'm just a cockeyed optimist?" (G. Bensusan, e-mail, June 17, 1996)
* "In a few years DL [distance learning] will be considered going to a campus and knowledge locally will be the expected norm—like the printing press, the electronic world will force traditional campuses to reorganize themselves and try to understand why someone should come to a campus for a DL experience. . . . Faculty will become like sports teams—a few super stars and a large number of team players filling different roles." (T. Ables, e-mail, July 22, 1996)
* "When comparing the relative advantages and dis-advantages of DE (Distance Education) and on-site programs, the DE program seems to have one major systemic drawback. Accessing periodicals is not

simple a matter of strolling over to the library. . . . As one following, rather gingerly, the footsteps of the sophists, I can say that the
Web is a useful teaching tool. I can park my tent where I like and
draw upon a tremendous range of materials." (P. A. K. Harper,
e-mail, July 10, 1996)

* "Technology contributes to conflicting future scenarios for higher
education. We can choose to ignore developments like the Western
Governors' University. . . . We can fight boundary-spanning satellite instruction, and try to establish signal-jamming Maginot Line
policies which prevent other institutions from getting a foothold
nearby—for a while. We can ignore the chorus of malcontents who
trash higher education and who propose technology box-top solu-
tions to complex problems—a bit longer. If we follow that strategy,
public higher education will begin to be seen like a rock in a river.
Events will flow around us, wearing us down in the process.
Campuses will become smaller, poorer, and more marginal to the
social mainstream. A more optimistic future is to embrace, not
reject, the use of new technologies. Use them to do what many
institutions have wanted to do anyway: Examine our strengths and
weaknesses and improve education for our community. Use technology to create new learning environments both on and off the
campus, environments which let students and faculty learn together.
Free professors from being confined to the role of "sage on the
stage," the tedious requirement to be experts in a world of information that is growing too quickly to totally comprehend. . . . Some
see the new technologies as the quaint teaching machines of the
1960s reborn in silicon clothing. . . . But higher education ignores
developments like the Western Governors' University at its own
peril." (R. M. Threlkeld, e-mail via G. Bensusan, July 12, 1996)

* "What I would like to see, in the structure of universities, is this:
I could be enrolled in the university where I am. I could make use
of their facilities (computer labs, student services, etc.), as I need
them. I could take any courses that they offer, either in person or
by distance, according to the subject and my own scheduling needs.
I could also take courses from any other school (or at least any other
in the system), by taking them though distance learning means. I could
use the help of the degree advisors at my school to develop my
program, coordinate my classes, and put together my disserta-
tion/project. I could graduate from my school." (M. Owen, e-mail,
July 26, 1996, relaying information he was given by one of his
students regarding long distance classes)

The Western Governors' University (WGU) is the newest innova-
tion among several western states. As of this writing the WGU will

have its headquarters in Denver, Colorado, and Salt Lake City, Utah, with sites or hubs in various places in each state. Idaho's hub will be in Idaho Falls at University Place. The WGU's mission is to extend and share educational courses throughout the western United States. Courses could be offered via distance learning through various links to colleges and universities, on-line courses through the Internet, satellite, and other technology that has not even been developed yet. At first glance, the WGU is one of the most technologically innovative methods of delivering and sharing among a multitude of educational institutions courses and curricula ever before imagined. Although various educators, including professors at the WGU colleges and universities, claim the WGU is part of a plot to deteriorate higher education, the majority of the players see the WGU as another wonderful option to disseminate knowledge that has been delivered in-house.

POINTS TO REMEMBER

* Distance professors have various opinions about the delivery of distance learning courses.
* Professors believe we could use technology more efficiently.

11

Conclusions, Recommendations, and Reflections

In this chapter we summarize the previous chapters. We also recommend to graduate students particular short-cuts—legal ones!—that will enable them to become more successful in completing their graduate programs via long distance. Questions to be contemplated follow.

* Now that I have read this book, what should I have learned?
* How can I use this book effectively?
* What other conclusions or recommendations can I make about the material?
* How can I take this information and use it in my own life?
* Are there topics that need further research?

Granted, distance education is not a panacea for all education. It is an additional tool whereby learners can "plug in to" another system of learning. It allows opportunities never before offered. Some people will scoff at the idea because of their traditional idealism. However, we believe that distance learning will become traditional idealism in a few years. In 5 to 10 years, we will be doing things never before imagined, just because people said to themselves, "I wonder if we can do this."

Problems and challenges will continue to rise and fall and become lost in the maze of WWW address and URLs. Colleges and universities have not completely decided how they are going to share degree programs, credits, students, ideas, courses, and so forth. A participant from the DEOS-L group asked, "How do the proponents of this way of doing things propose to get universities past their territorial, provincial, proprietary selves?" (J. Wang, e-mail, June 30, 1996). Wang also stated, "My suspicion is that interchange of programs and credits will start with a few small 'third-echelon' universities who want to leverage their programs. Eventually, more and more universities will join the network until the network can provide more choice and better programs than any one university possibly could. Holdouts will face the choice of allowing interchange of credits or dying." We concur with these thoughts, and add that we feel that the technology that is available today will truly bring the free enterprise system to the ivory towers of higher education.

Overall, our survey respondents enjoyed the entire process of long distance learning. Comments include,

* "Long distance course work made this degree possible. I could not have reached this goal any other way."
* "My program is definitely helping me translate my learning to on-the-job application."
* "I believe the entire aspect of completing a PhD while working full-time and teaching one class per semester and doing family things, etc., was grueling, yet fulfilling."
* "I thoroughly enjoyed the process. Most important factor for success was keeping up the momentum. I would highly recommend it. I felt I learned much more than in traditional learning setting. My program was totally self-directed. There were no scheduled classes except for an orientation of 3 weeks at the beginning. Within the prescribed framework I designed my adult education learning plan. It was approved by my advisor and the rest was up to me. I set my own time frames and designed my own learning plan. . . . The only time requirement was to complete the requirements within 5 years. The freedom of setting my own time frames enhanced my learning. I scheduled my learning time at the most convenient times for me—You can't do this in scheduled classes, and this can limit learning."

During the process of gathering the information for this book, we thought of several questions that would be of interest for further research:

* Is there a difference in the rates of students who complete graduate programs using long distance programs and those who complete graduate programs on campus?
* Is there a difference in divorce or separation rates among married students enrolled in distance graduate programs and those who complete graduate programs on campus?
* Is there a significant difference in the mean age of a graduate student participating in a distance learning program and the mean age of a graduate student participating in an on campus program?
* Is there a measurable difference in the mental health of a graduate student between the time of being enrolled in a graduate program and the time after graduation? In other words, do our so called post-dissertation blues actually exist?
* Is there a difference in the motivation levels of graduate students enrolled in a distance learning program and those enrolled in an on-campus program?
* Do distance graduate students have a greater level of self-reliance?
* Why do distance graduate students continue to enroll in classes?

We are certain that there are many more research questions to be answered. Perhaps you will think of them as you travel the journey along the distance learning path.

REFLECTIONS

There you have it, succinct and informal, straight from the mouths of those who actually have gone through a long distance learning graduate program and professors who actually teach at distance learning sites.

Granted, this is not theoretical, formalized information. When we review the data from the questionnaire, it is imperative that we remember our goal was not to conduct a scientific study or theorize but rather to gather some information from our colleagues about what they experienced as graduate students in a long distance graduate program. We wanted to hear it from those who actually participated in these types of programs. Theory is nice, but true experiences and perceptions help us as well. Often, emotive personal stories tell us more about what is going on in the real world.

Regardless of the delivery system of your graduate program, it will take considerable time to complete. Those of you who work full-time and have families will most likely feel overwhelmed at the thought of completing a degree part-time over a period of 3 to 5 years. We understand these feelings. But as we say to our colleagues who are contemplating enrolling in a doctoral program, "One thing is for certain, the next 5 years will go by whether or not I am in school. I'd like to be able to say that I completed a graduate degree, rather than I could have, if I had started."

Completing graduate school long distance is different than being on a regular campus and having access to everything within walking distance, as we have emphasized throughout this book. Long distance graduate school allows participants to be more creative in finding access to on-line services, contact graduate school personnel, and graduate committees. It should encourage you to reflect seriously on your relationships with your family, friends, and work. You have to say "no"once in a while.

A most important concept that escaped many of the members of our cohort group was the idea of finalizing a topic for study early in their program of study. In Steve's case, he did not decide on a topic until he had completed all but the final semester of coursework. If one can accomplish the task of establishing a topic early, it will allow you a greater amount of time to do the literature review. In addition, if you work it right, the research that is conducted in other classes during your program may be used as part of your study.

Overall, completing graduate school long distance, for us anyway, was exactly what we needed to do. It was the most appropriate educational avenue at the time. For you, it may be another story. This book is to help you make and confirm your decision to complete a graduate program long distance. Whatever you choose, we wish you good luck. If we can help you in any way, let us know. Happy commuting to graduate school—whether it be on campus, off campus in front of an interactive television, via satellite or videotapes, or sitting in front of your computer hooked on-line to some interactive classroom. No matter what happens, your graduate program will be unique. You deserve no less.

POINTS TO REMEMBER

- Distance education will become more widely accepted in the near future.
- The choices that are available to you now are few compared to those that will be available in the coming years.
- Schools will struggle with territorialism and compete for students. The free enterprise system is about to begin in the education community.

APPENDIX A

DEOS-L LISTSERV GRADUATE SCHOOLS THAT OFFER GRADUATE PROGRAMS VIA DISTANCE LEARNING

COLLEGES AND UNIVERSITIES THAT OFFER GRADUATE DISTANCE LEARNING COURSES IN THE UNITED STATES

The following list was posted to the DEOS-L listserv on July 17, 1996.

* Acadia University: teacher education
* Arizona State University: computer science, engineering, liberal arts/general studies

* Ball State University: accounting, business/management, teacher education
* Boise State University: instructional and performance technology
* California Institute of Integral Studies: liberal arts/general studies
* California State University, Chico: computer science, teacher education
* California State, Dominguez Hills: teacher education
* California State, Los Angeles: engineering, teacher education
* California State, Northridge: teacher education
* California State, Sacramento: business administration
* Chadron State College: business/management, teacher education
* College of Great Falls: social work
* Colorado State University: accounting, business/management, computer science, engineering, teacher education
* Corpus Christie State University: nursing
* Eastern Oregon State College: teacher education
* Embry-Riddle Aeronautical University: aeronautics
* Florida Atlantic University: business/management, engineering, teacher education
* Florida State University: electrical engineering, mechanical engineering
* George Washington University: business/management, computer science, engineering, teacher education
* Georgia Institute of Technology: engineering
* Governors' State University: allied health, liberal arts/general studies, teacher education
* Grand Valley State University: teacher education
* Indiana State University: environmental health and safety, human resource development, industrial technical education, teacher education
* Iowa State University of Science and Technology: agriculture, engineering, teacher education
* Kansas State University: agriculture, business/management, liberal arts/general studies
* Lehigh University: engineering, environmental health and safety, teacher education
* Mary Washington College: business administration, engineering
* Murray State University: accounting, allied health, business/management, nursing, teacher education
* National Technological University: computer science, engineering, environmental health and safety, foreign languages

* New Jersey Institute of Technology: business/management, chemistry, computer science, engineering, environmental health and safety, mathematics, physics
* New York University: business/management, computer science
* North Dakota State University: teacher education
* Northern Arizona University: education
* Oklahoma State University: accounting, business management, computer science, engineering, liberal arts/general studies
* Old Dominion University: accounting, allied health, business management, computer science, engineering, environmental health and safety, liberal arts/general studies, nursing, teacher education
* Oregon State University: engineering, environmental health and safety, teacher education
* Pennsylvania State University: allied health, engineering
* Portland State University: social work, teacher education
* Purdue University: engineering
* Regent University: accounting, biblical studies, business/ management
* Rensselaer Polytechnic Institute: business/management, computer science, engineering, technical communication
* Rice University: engineering
* Rochester Institute of Technology: computer science
* Salve Regina University: accounting, business/management, criminal justice/law, international relations, liberal arts/general studies
* San Jose State University: teacher education
* Southern Methodist University: computer science, engineering
* Southern Oregon State College: business/management, liberal arts/ general studies, teacher education
* Texas Tech University: higher education, teacher education
* University of Alabama: business/management, communications, computer science, engineering
* University of Alaska: teacher education
* University of Arizona: engineering, library science, pharmacy, teacher education
* University of Calgary: engineering, teacher education
* University of California, Santa Barbara: engineering
* University of Colorado, Boulder: business/management, computer science, engineering, environmental health and safety, telecommunications
* University of Colorado, Colorado Springs: accounting, engineering, space studies, teacher education
* University of Delaware: engineering

* University of Houston: engineering, liberal arts/general studies, teacher education
* University of Idaho: computer science, engineering
* University of Illinois: engineering
* University of Iowa: computer science, liberal arts/general studies, nursing, social work, teacher education
* University of Kentucky: agriculture, engineering, family studies, library science, nursing, pharmacy, teacher education
* University of Massachusetts: business/management, computer science, engineering, environmental health and safety, nursing
* University of Missouri: computer science, engineering
* University of Montana: accounting, public administration, teacher education
* University of Nebraska: business/management, computer science, engineering, teacher education
* University of New Brunswick: business/management, nursing, teacher education
* University of North Carolina: library science
* University of North Dakota: teacher education
* University of South Carolina: business/management, criminal justice/law, engineering, liberal arts/general studies, library and information science, nursing, public health, social work, teacher education

Although this list represents various colleges and universities, it does not represent all institutions by the time this book goes to publication. We have discovered that technology progresses faster than we can keep up. Moreover, colleges and universities are jumping into the educational fray as rapidly as they can in order to keep up with the competition. As long as students request on-line courses and as long as technology provides a vehicle that makes it easier and easier for educational entities to develop courses on-line, then the proliferation of courses on-line will spread across the wires. Of course, we applaud the movement. But we caution you as well to use a jaundiced eye when researching for a graduate school. Remember, accreditation is a big deal, and valid universities and colleges will be accredited by the appropriate accrediting entity in their service area. Again, be watchful and judicious when selecting a graduate school completely on-line. You will not regret it.

APPENDIX B

GLOBEWIDE NETWORK ACADEMY CATALOG

The following is a list of other colleges that offer long distance learning programs, both graduate and undergraduate, from the Globewide Network Academy Catalog, http://catalog.gnacademy.org/cgi-bin/cg, as of August 29, 1996

INSTITUTION AND
NUMBER OF PROGRAMS

- American Academy of Nutrition: 2 Programs, 21 Courses
- American College of Prehospital: 3 Programs, 30 Courses
- American Military University: 1 Program, 135 Courses
- Anglia Polytechnic University, Division of Radiography: 5 Programs
- Arapahoe Community College: 1 Program
- Athabasca University: 2 Programs, 322 Courses
- Athena University: 10 Programs, 347 Courses

* Atlantic Union College: 2 Programs
* Auburn University: 12 Programs, 16 Courses
* Bastyr University: 2 Programs
* Boise State University: 1 Program; College of Technology: 6 Courses
* Brigham Young University: 3 Programs, 524 Courses
* CAL Campus: 3 Programs
* CHAT and SHARE: 1 Program
* CHOICE 2000 On-2DLine school: 2 Programs
* California Coast University: 12 Programs
* California College for Health Sciences: 7 Programs
* California National University: 14 Programs
* California State University: 2 Programs
* Cambrian College: 4 Programs
* Central Michigan University: 14 Programs, 44 Courses
* Charter Oak State College: 12 Programs
* City University EDROADS: 1 Program
* Clarkson College: 2 Programs
* Cleveland State University: 1 Program in Health Care Administration
* Colorado State University: 14 Programs, 44 Courses [New]
* Columbia Pacific University: 4 Programs
* Columbia Union College: 6 Programs
* Connected Education: 1 Program
* East Carolina University Technology: 1 Program, 2 Courses
* Edith Cowan University: 1 Program, 4 Courses
* Embry—Riddle Aeronautical University: 2 Programs
* Empire State College—State University of New York: 18 Programs
* Escuela Bancaria y Comercial, Mexico: 3 Programs
* Fielding Institute: 6 Programs
* Flinders University of South Australia: 2 Programs
* Front Range Community College: 1 Program, 20 Courses
* George Washington University: 1 Program
* Georgia Institute of Technology: 5 Programs
* Goddard College: 20 Programs
* Governors' State University: 1 Program
* Graduate School of America: 4 Programs, 136 Courses
* Graduate School of the United States: 7 Programs, 115 Courses
* Department of Agriculture, Greenwich University: 6 Programs
* Henson College of Dalhousie University: 7 Programs

* Heriot-Watt University: 1 Program
* Heritage Institute, Antioch University: 1 Program, 17 Courses
* ICI University: 3 Programs
* Indiana State University: 1 Program, 256 Courses
* Institute of Education, University of London: 1 Program
* Intec College: 5 Programs, 54 Courses
* International Correspondence Schools: 10 Programs
* International School of Information: 2 Programs
* International University College: 5 Programs
* Iowa State Engineering Distance Education: 15 Programs
* Judson College: 11 Programs
* Kansas State University: 2 Programs, 34 Courses
* Memorial University of Newfoundland: 8 Programs, 48 Courses
* Metropolitan State College of Denver: 18 Courses [New]
* Microsoft On-line Institute: 3 Programs
* Mindquest: 1 Program
* National Academy of Mortuary Science: 1 Program
* National Institute of Paralegal Arts and Sciences: 2 Programs
* National Technological University: 1 Program
* New Jersey Institute of Technology: 1 Program
* New School for Social Research: 2 Programs, 85 Courses
* North Carolina State University: 1 Program
* Northeastern State University, Oklahoma: 1 Program
* Northwestern College: 3 Programs, 48 Courses
* Nova Southeastern University: 10 Programs
* Ohio University: 6 Programs, 188 Courses
* On-line Education: 5 Programs
* Open University, Orlando, Florida: 7 Programs
* Open University, United Kingdom: 32 Programs, 2 Courses
* Pennsylvania State University: 16 Programs, 198 Courses
* Prescott College: 15 Programs
* Regent University: 7 Programs, 12 Courses
* Regis University: 1 Program
* Rhodec International: 2 Programs
* Rochester Institute of Technology: 19 Programs
* Rogers State College: 5 Programs, 29 Courses
* Saybrook Institute: 4 Programs
* Simon Fraser University: 6 Programs, 74 Courses

- Skidmore College: 33 Programs
- Stephens College: 7 Programs
- Sun Microsystems: 1 Program, 94 Courses
- Syracuse University: 12 Programs
- Taylor University: 2 Programs, 71 Courses
- Texas A&M University: 11 Programs, 11 Courses
- Thomas Edison State College: 15 Programs
- Union Institute: 10 Programs
- United Nations Trade Point: 2 Programs
- United States Sports Academy: 1 Program, 35 Courses
- University of Aberystwyth, Wales: 9 Programs
- University of Alaska Southeast: 1 Program
- University of Arizona: 1 Program
- University of Bath: 9 Programs
- University of British Columbia: 5 Programs, 97 Courses
- University of Colorado CATECS: 6 Programs, 127 Courses
- University of Colorado at Colorado Springs: 2 Programs, 4 Courses
- University of Delaware: 3 Programs, 90 Courses
- University of Dundee: 3 Programs
- University of Florida: 1 Program, 121 Courses
- University of Georgia: 6 Programs, 135 Courses
- University of Idaho Engineering: 8 Programs
- University of Iowa: 1 Program, 164 Courses
- University of La Verne: 1 Program
- University of Maine: 1 Program
- University of Maryland: 9 Programs
- University of Massachusetts at Amherst: 4 Programs
- University of North Dakota: 1 Program, 79 Courses
- University of North Dakota Corporate: 3 Programs
- University of Oklahoma: 3 Programs, 178 Courses
- University of Pennsylvania: 1 Program
- University of Phoenix: 6 Programs
- University of South Florida: 1 Program
- University of Southern Colorado: 2 Programs, 81 Courses
- University of Strathclyde in Glasgow: 3 Programs
- University of Surrey: 3 Programs
- University of Wyoming: 1 Program, 95 Courses
- Upper Iowa University: 11 Programs, 71 Courses

- Vermont College of Norwich University: 120 Programs
- Virtual School of Monterey Institute of Technology: 10 Programs
- Walden University: 5 Programs
- Washington State University: 1 Program, 153 Courses
- Western Illinois University: 1 Program, 98 Courses
- Wuhan University, People's Republic of China: 1 Program
- Wyoming College of Advanced Studies: 1 Program

References and Bibliography

Directory of Postsecondary Institutions. (1997). Washington, DC: National Center for Education Statistics, U.S. Department of Education.

Dixon, P. (1996). *Virtual college: A quick guide to how you can get the degree you want with computer, TV, video, audio, and other distance learning tools.* Princeton, NJ: Peterson's.

Duffy, J. P. (1994). *How to earn an advanced degree without going to graduate school.* 2nd ed. New York: John Wiley & Sons.

Ellis, D. (1994). *Becoming a master student.* 7th ed. Boston: Houghton Mifflin.

The electronic university: A guide to distance learning programs. (1993). Princeton, NJ: Peterson's Guides.

Longman, D. G., & Atkinson, R. H. (1993). *College learning and study skills.* 3rd ed. St. Paul, MN: West.

Higher Education Directory. (1986). Falls Church, VA: Higher Education Publications.

Peterson's guide to distance learning. (1996). Princeton, NJ: Peterson's. (Formerly *The Electronic University*)

Rossman, M. H. (1995). *Negotiating graduate school: A guide for graduate students.* Thousand Oaks, CA: Sage Publications.

Rudestam, K. E., & Newton, R. R. (1992). *Surviving your dissertation: A comprehensive guide to content and process.* Newbury Park, CA: Sage Publications.

Stewart, D., & Spille, H. A. (1988). *Diploma mills: Degrees of fraud.* Washington, DC: American Council on Education.

Thorson, M. K. (1996). *Campus-free college degrees.* Holbrook: Adams Media.

INDEX

ABOUT THE AUTHORS

Darrel L. Hammon, PhD, grew up in Menan, Idaho, graduated from Boise State University with a BA in English and an MA in English Education, and received his PhD in Education with an Adult Education emphasis from the University of Idaho. He is currently the Associate Vice-President for Extended Programs and Community Development at Lewis-Clark State College in Lewiston, Idaho. He has also taught undergraduate English and graduate vocational teacher and adult education courses at Idaho State University and University of Idaho. He writes regularly for the *Post Register* and is working on two books. In addition, he is the President of the Idaho Lifelong Learning Association (ILLA).

Steven K. Albiston, PhD, grew up in the rural community of St. Anthony, Idaho, graduated from the University of Idaho with a BS in Psychology, MEd in Guidance and Counseling, and a PhD in Education with an Adult Education emphasis. He is currently the Dean of Students at Eastern Idaho Technical College. He has been active in professional organizations as a Past President of the Idaho Association of Collegiate Registrars and Admissions Officers and the Idaho Career Development Association. He is the Immediate Past Chairperson of the Idaho State Guidance Advisory Committee and received the 1996 Idaho Vocational Association's Idaho Vocational Counselor Educator Award.